MW00436712

ALIVE
TO THE
PURPOSE

THE READERLY
READING
OF SCRIPTURE

RONALD A. HORTON

journeyforth®

Greenville, South Carolina

Library of Congress Cataloging-in Publication Data
Names: Horton, Ronald Arthur, 1936¬ author.
Title: Alive to the purpose : the readerly reading of scripture / Ronald A.
 Horton.
Description: Greenville, South Carolina : BJU Press, 2020. | Summary:
 "Alive to the Purpose is an examination of how to read Scripture without an
 agenda, instead allowing the text to bring to us the richness of the divinely
 inspired story" — Provided by publisher.
Identifiers: LCCN 2019055956 (print) | LCCN 2019055957 (ebook) |
 ISBN 9781628569742 (paperback) | ISBN 9781628569759 (eISBN)
Subjects: LCSH: Bible—Reading. | Bible—Appreciation.
Classification: LCC BS617 .H63 2020 (print) | LCC BS617 (ebook) |
 DDC 220.601—dc23
LC record available at https://lccn.loc.gov/2019055956
LC ebook record available at https://lccn.loc.gov/2019055957

All Scripture is quoted from the King James Version. Italicized words in Scripture passages indicate the emphasis of the author.

The fact that materials produced by other publishers may be referred to in this volume does not constitute an endorsement of the content or theological position of materials produced by such publishers.

Alive to the Purpose is published posthumously by JourneyForth Books based on the author's work in progress.

Editor: Nancy Lohr
Designer: Elly Kalagayan
Page layout: Michael Boone

© 2020 BJU Press
Greenville, South Carolina 29609
JourneyForth Books is a division of BJU Press.

Printed in the United States of America
All rights reserved

ISBN 978-1-62856-974-2
eISBN 978-1-62856-975-9

15   14   13   12   11   10   9   8   7   6   5   4   3   2   1

For as the rain cometh down, and the snow from heaven,
and returneth not thither, but watereth the earth,
and maketh it bring forth and bud,
that it may give seed to the sower, and bread to the eater:
So shall my word be that goeth forth out of my mouth:
it shall not return unto me void,
but it shall accomplish that which I please,
and it shall prosper in the thing whereto I sent it.

Isaiah 55:10–11

CONTENTS

FOREWORD

Ron Horton was an acknowledged scholar in the field of English Language and Literature, proved by the various articles and books he authored. Because of his specialty in Edmund Spenser's *The Faerie Queen*, he needed more than a passing acquaintance with philosophical and religious concepts. This interest led him later in life to focus on philosophy and worldview issues. Thereby our lives intertwined since the philosophy courses he taught were housed in the School of Religion, of which I was dean. (And, by the way, his wife Martha had been my English tutorial instructor when I was a freshman in college!)

Ron was one of my faculty members, and I got to know him quite well. He was a humble giant, characterized by prodigious learning but always self-effacing and open to being taught. He visited my office regularly (and always apologized for intruding and wasting my time, although I was most assuredly the beneficiary of each visit) to bounce ideas off my head, to share something he had learned, or to pass along an article that pertained to biblical studies. He was especially burdened that men training for the ministry (as well as lay people in general) not get bogged down by a solely academic study of the Bible. Ron most definitely did not espouse a nonacademic approach to God's Word, evidenced by his use of biblical language word studies, technical background material, and literary styles. However, he warned that important points could be missed or overlooked if all our Bible study focused on microscopic detail. He opted, rather, for the nonintentional reading of the Bible for both pleasure and profit. Of course, he had a leg up on most of us in this regard because of his grasp of literary skills and concepts. However, he maintained that any believer being Spirit indwelt, could, by reading thoughtfully and curiously with faculties on high alert and mental powers engaged, come to a deeper understanding of the Bible.

Thus in this book you get a taste of how to read the Bible nonintentionally. This is not a hermeneutics textbook (hermeneutics is the science of interpretation, and usually such textbooks give important principles on how to interpret or unlock the varied genres of literature in the Bible), although such are needful and valuable. Here Ron takes us by the hand and leads us through varied texts—Samuel, Kings, Psalms, the Gospels, Romans, Hebrews, and more—to illustrate fine nuances we probably never considered and to "see" things we would never find in a dozen commentaries. Because of his daily walk with the Lord over many decades, his familiarity with the Bible's stories enables him to seamlessly piece together contrasts and comparisons. And Ron is always quick to bring the reader to the realization of how the passage applies to his life. God is still speaking through His Word to us!

Such an exhortation to read the Bible for pleasure and profit is needed today. Too many Christians are flippant or casual in handling God's Word. They read "a verse a day to keep the devil away" or look for a verse to serve as a "power pill" to get through the events of the day or confine their reading to only a few select passages in Psalms or the New Testament. Ron's gentle coaxing helps us see the Bible's story line and how the individual stories all contribute to it. This requires a continuous (all the time) and comprehensive (all the Bible) reading plan, as God honors those who honor Him. Therefore, Ron wants us to share in his love for the Bible, and thus for the Bible's Author.

Augustine (AD 354–430), one of the early church fathers, spent the first three decades of his life in profligacy and in bondage to lust, conceit, vanity, and heretical sects of Christianity. However, one day in August, AD 386, as he was walking in a garden in a great turmoil of soul, he heard the voice of a child in a nearby house chanting and repeating, "Take up and read, take up and read." So he went back into the house, picked up a Bible, and read the first passage he opened to, which was Romans 13:13–14.[1] These verses command one to put off the old sinful self and all its vanities and to put on Christ. At that moment he confessed he passed from darkness to light, and his life was never the same!

Ron's desire for us would also be that we "take up and read." This book? Perhaps. But most of all that we would consistently and comprehensively and curiously read God's Book. It will transform our lives and be one of God's agents to conform us into the likeness of Jesus Christ.

Royce Short, PhD
Former Dean of the School of Religion, Bob Jones University
Greenville, South Carolina

---

1. Edward B. Pusey, trans., *The Confessions of St. Augustine* (New York: P. F. Collier & Son, 1909), VIII, 141–143.

INTRODUCTION

The Bible is more often studied and searched and scrutinized and analyzed and theologized and memorized and dipped into and skimmed and scanned—all worthy and important actions—than it is *read*, that is *really read*.

This state of affairs comes to us from the top down. The *formal study* of Scripture tends in scholarly exegesis and commentary toward microanalysis on the one hand—that is, to discrete minuteness—or on the other hand toward abstraction—the clarifying and arranging of belief statements as in systematic theology.

Likewise, on the *common level* (or the informal study) there is the blessing-for-the-day approach with selected inspirational nuggets, favoring a particled engagement with Scripture. There is also the practical life-directed approach, mining Scripture for governing principles, pursuing general concepts and favoring abstraction. The Bible welcomes these approaches. It *is* a treasury of rich minutiae and connectable, applicable truths. But it is much more.

The Bible is so constituted that it provides for and encourages a diversity of approaches that serve a diversity of needs. The formal study of Scripture yields knowledge and skills essential to accurate understanding and exegesis. The less formal approaches minister to the soul during personal times alone with God as well as in the gathered group. But what can get left out, what tends to fall through the cracks, is simply *reading*—what goes on when our attention is clenched to a page, captivated by a line of thought, adventuring within a biblical scene or situation we have staged in our minds.

The Bible, in the way many Christians read, remains under a glass case—indeed a special case—to be read in a way all its own with learned guidance. It *is* that most certainly—a special book to be read in a special way. But it is also a special book to be read in a non-special way—that is, to be read thoughtfully with an interest that carries us forward with eagerness and rapt attention. Even when the Bible is perused daily and conscientiously from Genesis to Revelation or according to another plan, as well it should be, what can get slighted—in the effort to cover, say, the obligatory three chapters and a Psalm—is reflective reading. We can do our daily duty and set the Book aside, forgetful that the Bible may be read, in fact should be read, with all our mental powers employed.

Readerly reading allows the Bible to interest us in the same way a well-chosen story does. This can get forgotten—if ever learned—in the humdrum, pressured business of life. To read in a readerly fashion is to devour a well-crafted story with pleasure. No less a master of narrative than Ernest Hemingway once said that the best stories ever written (for artistry and intrinsic interest) are to be found in the history books of the Old Testament. How might he have come up with that? Well, he was reading these stories as literature, wasn't he? And we know for sure Bible stories are not literature, don't we? They are inspired examples meant for our learning, not for our pleasure, aren't they? And so we assure ourselves that in Scripture the didactic and the pleasurable are at odds, that reading Bible stories for enjoyment is for children. Right?

Well, no. We are wrong, and our error comes with a cost. We deprive ourselves of what writers of stories have always known: that what we call literature can serve serious purpose in powerful ways. The poet W. H. Auden invoked an old distinction between art that instructs and art that entertains and restores. "There must always be two kinds of art, escape-art, for man needs escape as he needs food and deep sleep, and parable art, that art which shall teach man to unlearn hatred and learn love."[2] The two purposes can dovetail. Pleasure and serious purpose can meet in our reading of God's Word. In fact we diminish that reading experience when we fail to bring to it the skills and readiness in play when we read what is less necessary to our growth in God.

Benjamin Franklin, when serving as American ambassador to France, enjoyed the social life of Paris while soliciting French support for the Colonies in their war against Britain. His witty conversation diverted the court but also made him popular in the intellectual salons of the city. On one visit, Franklin, a great tease, asked those assembled whether they would like to hear a charming oriental story from long ago.

With their eager assent, the canny statesman proceeded to tell them a suspenseful tale of a love plot enacted with high risk under cover of darkness by a young widow woman, put up to it by her mother-in-law, seeking a well-to-do husband who had noticed her in his field. Everything had to go exactly right if the stratagem were to succeed and if a horrible embarrassment, indeed disabling shame, were to be avoided. Ruth dressed and anointed herself as a bride, slipped into the tent of the sleeping workers, and slid under the man's robe.

Franklin's audience, open despisers of religion, were mesmerized—and no less amazed when informed by Franklin, with no doubt a straight face, that the story was to be found in the Bible. Franklin's listeners were responding to the story with all their faculties, their natural faculties, alive.

The Scriptures in their entirety tell a story. There are deep currents. Whether, for example, we think forward from the Old Testament to the New in biblical theology or extend backward from the New Testament to the Old in systematic theology affects our weighting of the parts. Every piece is backlit by the grand narrative—from separation to restoration, from farness to nearness, from loss to reclamation, with gracious solicitation of

---

2. Peter Edgerly Firchow. *W. H. Auden: Contexts for Poetry*. (Danvers, MA: Rosemont Publishing & Printing Corp., 2002), 134.

fallen beings at both ends, a fallen Cain among them. But that will not be our primary interest here.

We will attend to the pieces, and as we consider them, we will mind the story and the story line, alive to the purpose, for no other religion has a divinely inspired story like ours.

PART 1

READING THE STORY

The Bible is a special book to be read thoughtfully with a curiosity that carries us forward with eagerness. We should read with all our faculties fully focused and alive to the literary pursuit, exercising the same skills and readiness we use when we read works less important to our growth in God.

1

CONNECT WITH
OTHER PASSAGES

Notice how much is revealed of the Son of God in John's account of the Last Supper when we read for the story. Chapter 13 opens with the observation that Jesus, knowing His time of departure was come, "having loved his own which were in the world, he loved them unto the end"[1] (v. 1). We notice Jesus loving His disciples, in an intensely focused way, during His final hours before the crucifixion. He interrupts the meal ("supper being ended" in verse 2 seems not the best translation) to give the disciples an object lesson. It is in preparation for an important commandment He will leave with them. He performs for each of them—Judas included—a task allotted to slaves, if done at all. He kneels before them with a towel and a basin of water.

Outspoken Peter objects. His Master must not demean Himself so. Jesus tells Peter that unless he be washed he cannot be His disciple. Peter says, "Well then, wash all of me." Jesus replies that after one is washed he needs only to wash his feet, being "clean every whit," adding cryptically, "and ye are clean, but not all" (v. 10). The import of Jesus' action is that the disciples are

---

1. The author uses the King James Version here and throughout for its tonalities, concreteness, and thumping reinforcement of meaning.

to bend to one another in love as He has bent to them in loving service. "If I then, your Lord and Master, have washed your feet; ye also ought to wash one another's feet" (v. 14).

Now Jesus enlarges what He has just intimated of there being a pretender among His disciples: "I speak not of you all: I know whom I have chosen. . . . [One of you will lift] up his heel against me" (v.18). He is informing them in advance so they won't be taken by surprise and think He also is taken by surprise. After a separate observation about His oneness with His messengers, He appears "troubled in spirit" (v. 21) and declares with emphasis that one of them will be His betrayer. The disciples naturally are shaken and look at each other anxiously. Their little group seems to be disintegrating. The Lord Himself has been wrenched by what He has said—and said with painful reluctance. Jesus knew the shattering potential of Judas's departure on the disciples. He felt the blow Himself. He loved Judas and knew they did too.

After Judas's dismissal, Jesus is with His true followers, and He is going to make use of their final hours together. In her account of her childhood and youth during the Russian persecution in her book *Children of the Storm*, Natasha Vins describes her father's few minutes alone with the family before he is taken away. He takes the children aside one by one and tells them the things he wants them to remember, not the least of which is his love. It is a charged scene. There is great unsettlement in the listeners, with intense purpose and affection in the words directed to them. Their minds are locked together. Their hearts are pounding.[2]

In much the same way, a reader who brings his imagination into play reading the thirteenth chapter in John's Gospel will feel the intensity of the moment, its crucial importance, and the emotions engaged. Jesus tells His eleven the time has come for Him to be glorified. He would have them look beyond the dark event about to take place to its bright conclusion. The Son will

---

2. Natasha Vins. *Children of the Storm.* (Greenville, SC: BJU Press, 2002), xi–xiii.

be glorified by the Father, and the Father glorified in the Son. In this encouraging context He sets forth the blunt fact that they will soon be without Him and that where He is they cannot go. But He is not abandoning His headship. He is leaving them with a commandment of the highest importance. It is "a new commandment" that He has just illustrated in the foot washing. "A new commandment I give unto you, That ye love one another; as I have loved you, that ye also love one another" (John 13:34). Their obedience to the new commandment will, in fact, be their primary identifying mark as His disciples. "By this shall all men know that ye are my disciples, if ye have love one to another" (v. 35).

This new commandment addresses their recent behavior, which we learn from the other Gospels has not been the best. It is the point the story has been building toward, an injunction necessary to be understood and retained. The commandment is *new* in that it goes beyond loving your neighbor as yourself, an Old Testament command repeated by the Lord earlier that final week. It goes beyond the Golden Rule iterated in the Sermon on the Mount (Matt. 7:12): that you do unto others what you would that others do unto you. The new commandment to the disciples is that they love one another as their Master has loved them (John 13:34), with a love rising above self-concern and having a divine rather than human benchmark. It is a huge requirement scarcely conceivable yet necessary to be grasped and retained. It goes to the heart of what the Lord is about to accomplish for them and for us all. How does it affect the listening disciples?

Peter blurts out, "Where are you going? Why can't I follow you? I will follow you." Jesus' weighted words had swept right by him. In his state of agitation, Peter did not hear the injunction, nor did the other disciples—except John, who perhaps at the very time he was penning this incident was also writing an epistle to emphasize it. At this point, the Lord, as a wise teacher, rather than driving His point, takes leave of it for the moment in order to deal with their fear and confusion. He addresses their state of mind.

They don't want Him to leave. They fear the separation. Their little group has stayed together for three and a half years. If they had needs, they asked Him. If they failed to understand what He had told the crowds, they questioned Him. If they were troubled, He comforted them. If they were sent by Him on a mission, He instructed them and empowered them and listened to their reports when they returned. What were they now to do? Go back to their families again? Fade back into ordinary life? He had called them to more than that. Little children have bouts of separation anxiety. So on a massive scale do the disciples here.

Jesus tells them not to let their "heart[s] be troubled" (14:1) and sets about to *untrouble* them. Yes, He indeed must leave them, but He is leaving them for their benefit. He will prepare a place for them. His Father has a big house with lots of rooms. He will bring them to that house in due time.

"How will we get there?" asks Thomas. "We don't know the way."

The Lord answers, "I am the way, the truth, and the life. You get there through me, and only through me."

"If we could just see this Father you have been speaking of, that would untrouble our minds," says Philip.

"Now Philip, have I been with you all this time and you still haven't known Me? If you've seen Me, you've seen My Father."

And then a climactic irony: He must leave them in order to return to them and serve them in fuller ways. He will send a Comforter who will always be present with them.

When Jesus was on a mountain praying or on the shore while they were rowing, He could not comfort them as He did when He was close enough for them to talk with Him as He was then. Having the Comforter with them to perform these functions would be better since the Comforter would always be at hand. That was not all. The Father Himself would be responding to their requests and enabling their works just as Jesus had done. Indeed—and this is amazing—Jesus must leave so not only the

Comforter but also the Father and He Himself could return and abide with them. The entire Godhead would take up residence with them in a constant, immediate, embracing way. It was a staggering thought that the love of the Father for the Son Jesus would extend to them also, that they would be drawn into the family love of the Trinity.

So though He would be leaving, He would be leaving only in His physical person, and from His leaving would accrue the full privileges of membership in the family of God, of which the chief identifier is mutual love. It was His peace and His joy, and He would leave it with them. He says again, "Let not your heart be troubled, neither let it be afraid" (14:27).

But Jesus was not through with this line of thought, nor should we be. The following chapter break obscures the continuity. Having dealt in chapter 14 with their fears of losing Him and quieting their minds to the point that He could teach them (yet teaching them important truths while in the act of quieting them), He reframed the issue. They did not want Him to leave; He must abide with them. But they need not worry. He Himself would return and abide with them. They were now of His family. Their real concern was not *His abiding with them*. That had been taken care of. It was *their abiding with Him*. And so there followed the parable of the vine and the branches in chapter 15.

Israel had been a false vine, neglected by its gardeners and ravaged by intruders. All the national failure—religious, political, and cultural—imaged in this emblem is to be displaced by what is assembled in that room and kindred followers. The Father is now the vine dresser. The health of the vine will no longer depend upon what is external to it. The owner of the vineyard will no longer rule from afar. The vine will be united to its divine source organically, and the strength of the vine will be communicated systemically to the branches through the divine root and stock—the Son of God. The divine vine dresser will clear away the worthless branches and prune or "clean" the good branches—"ye are clean, but not all" (13:10)—to increase their health and yield.

Their Master will abide with them. There need be no anxiety on that side. Their hearts need not be troubled on that account. Instead they must take to heart the real variable. They, the branches, must remain united with the vine.

Jesus' prayer for His disciples in John 17 reinforces what He has just taught them. It centers on their unity with one another and with the Father and Him. It summarizes what He has urged on them and shows the love of the persons of the Trinity extending to and embracing the disciples—the branches of the true vine—as well.

We have been following a story line. *What has it shown us about our God?* Surely His attentive affectionate care of His own. He has bent to them, not only in the physical act of washing their feet but also in taking momentary leave of their instruction on a subject of high importance in order to calm their fears. Both interruptions, of the supper and of the teaching of the New Commandment, are prompted by love. They also supplied essential truths for Jesus' disciples both then and now.

We have read for the story and learned something about our God that can reassure us as well as its original audience. We have also learned that what are called discourses in John may very well include audience interaction with links less obviously logical than psychological. Jesus is shown reacting to the responses of His listeners (their spoken replies or their mutterings or their unspoken thoughts) while still maintaining the direction of the teaching, even using their interruptions to motivate His argument.

Very possibly about the same time as he was writing the fourth Gospel, the elderly apostle was writing his three Epistles. The preeminent theme of 1 John is precisely that command of the Lord "that ye love one another, as I have loved you" found in John 15:12. It had been sorely needed before, and evidently from the Epistle's content was sorely needed then as well. John's next two epistles refine the theme of the first. Second John presents a case of *too much love*, an over-generous indiscriminate hospitality extended to *unworthy* itinerants. Third John speaks of *too little love*, a withholding of hospitality to a *worthy* itinerant.

Before leaving the writings of John, let us return to the Gospel and consider the ending. That is more easily said than done, for the Gospel of John has two endings: one in chapter 20, a summary by John of his story's intention, and the other in chapter 21, adding an episode that may seem tacked on but may also have a summarizing purpose. Let's look at the latter of the two with our imaginations in play. We'll take a bird's eye view while keeping alert for promising particulars.

In chapter 21 John records "the third time that Jesus shewed Himself to His disciples, after that he was risen from the dead" (21:14). He had told them He would meet them in Galilee after His resurrection, and in Galilee we find seven of them in accordance with their instructions somewhere near the place of their calling.

Peter has an impulse to return to his occupation. He was in business with the family of Zebedee, father of James and John. "I go a fishing," he says. The six follow his lead. "We also go with thee" (21:3). It's hard to say whether this amounts to a failure of faith. It is reasonable that he occupy himself with something positive he knew how to do while he waited. I think we should take a generous view of these disciples in their vulnerable time.

We know the story, or maybe mostly. Notice the art of the telling of it. Every detail counts. There is no wasted motion. Notice the contrast. They "entered into a ship *immediately; and that night they caught *nothing*." Nothing hurts more than providentially designed futility. But something was providentially happening on the shore. "When the morning was now come, Jesus stood on the shore" (v. 4).

Jesus wasn't yet recognized by the disciples in the boat. What wonderful suspense. He shouted to them, addressing them as "children," which should have been a giveaway, "Do you have any food?" The irony is beautiful. Notice the brevity of their reply. Can you imagine the tone of it? "They answered him, No" (v. 5). The irony enlarges. This stranger on the shore instructs them to do something incredibly absurd. "Cast the net on the right side of the ship, and ye shall find." Even more incredibly they do as He says. "They cast therefore, and now they were not able to draw it for the multitude of fishes" (v. 6).

Peter was dumbfounded. John tells Peter. "It is the Lord" (v. 7). John's understanding is ahead of Peter's as we have seen before. Running to the garden tomb, Peter was ahead of John; but when both got to the tomb, John's understanding outpaced Peter's. Once John identifies the Lord to Peter and the others, Peter physically as before will take the lead. "When Simon Peter heard that it was the Lord, he girt his fisher's coat unto him . . . and did cast himself into the sea" (v. 7). We can't help remembering another time when Peter in a boat with the other disciples took a walk upon the waves to meet his Lord (Matt. 14). This time he would swim and be more successful. What a lovely, simple man he shows himself to be. Give Peter time to get it all straight, and when he does . . . well, we'll find out in Acts.

The other disciples follow Peter to land, dragging the net since it was too filled with fish—153 in all (John 21:11), by Peter's count I suspect—to pull its contents into the boat. Burly Peter drags the net to the shore. Now the man on the shore, the Son of Man, moves to the center of the story, where of course He has been, though unrecognized, all along. And He will draw Peter to the center with Him.

Notice several fascinating details here. "As soon then as they were come to land, they saw a fire of coals there, and fish laid thereon" (21:9). Where before in John's Gospel have we seen "a fire of coals?" Peter would have recalled a time if we happen not to. His Lord "then cometh, and taketh bread, and giveth them, and fish likewise" (v. 13). Where in the wilderness would Jesus have located enough bread to go with the fish of these hungry fishermen? The disciples would remember two other times if we can't. Then John remarks "This is now the third time that Jesus shewed himself to his disciples, after that he was risen from the dead" (v. 14). John has us thinking in threes, following the facts of course.

Now back to that fire of coals. When Jesus was led bound into the palace of Annas the high priest, John who "was known unto the high priest" followed also (18:35). Peter was left standing at the door until John brought him in.

> Then saith the damsel that kept the door unto Peter, Art
> not thou also one of this man's disciples? He saith, I am not.
> And the servants and officers stood there, who had made a
> fire of coals; for it was cold . . . and Peter stood with them,
> [yes, he did] and warmed himself. (vv. 17–18)

Soon we read of the same question put to Peter in the high priest's courtyard standing by a fire.

> And Simon Peter stood and warmed himself. They said
> therefore unto him, Art not thou also one of his disciples?
> He denied it and said, I am not. (v. 25)

Then came the third and climactic question, Peter still by the fire, from one whom he would have special reason to fear. Peter had met him before.

> One of the servants of the high priest, being his kinsman
> whose ear Peter cut off, saith, Did not I see thee in the garden with him? (v. 26)

The questions were coming close to home. "Peter then denied again: and immediately the cock crew" (v. 27), announcing the dawn and confirming Peter's earlier emphatic denial, then spoken to his Savior, "Why cannot I follow thee now? I will lay down my life for thy sake" (13:37).

Jesus replied with equal emphasis, "Verily, verily, I say unto thee, The cock shall not crow, till thou has denied me thrice" (v. 38). It would be the saddest of all dawns Peter would ever know. But it would not of momentous dawns be the last for Peter. We will meet the coal fire again in that final encounter of Peter and the Lord in our story in John 21. After breakfast Jesus will take Peter aside and give him an opportunity to roll back the tape as it were and clear his soul of what has been forgiven him—those guilt feelings can linger on—in one of the most revealing incidents of God's love in all of Scripture. Psychology is at work too.

Peter has seen a figure standing on the shore of the lake identified for him by his friend John as the Lord, and he cannot resist swimming toward Him. We would know of Peter's grieving heart from this action even if we didn't know already of his heart's wounded condition. That fire of coals would signal to Peter the hope of a healing from the Great Physician. It is fascinating what followed.

Three times, one for each denial, Peter is asked by his Master whether he is one of His. No, not so much *whose he is*, but *who Peter loves*, truly loves. Peter's grief seems to mount with each affirming. But in the process his guilty feelings are in retreat. Peter is made to realize his own mastering love, that there is more hope for him as a disciple than he fears there might be after his triple denial in the high priest's courtyard by a fire of coals.

The self-realization of one's love of the Lord and of the Lord's own is a persuasive remedy of spiritual doubt given in 1 John 5— that a troubled saint is indeed part of the family. He loves God and what God loves rather than the reverse. The structuring of this interview to interact point by point is what I meant by the psychology of our loving, shrewd God who specializes in complicated needs.

This purging and commissioning of Peter is just right for a conclusion of John's story about Peter and Peter's future leadership. He was called to be a fisher of men, no longer of fish. His reverting to his former occupation is an occasion for his recommissioning, this one as an under shepherd of the Great Shepherd with a ministry to the saints. He would of course continue to be both. In Acts—at Pentecost and thereafter—Peter can be seen fishing for men. In those two remarkable epistles written years later, we see him in the role of his latter calling, the shepherding of God's sheep.

Thoughtful reading considers connections
between separate parts of Scripture.

2

REFLECT ON THE SETTING

An epistle is not a story, though it may contain stories; nor is it a treatise, though it may contain sections that are systematic like a treatise. Hebrews comes closest to being entirely a treatise. Let's consider Paul's Epistle to the Romans as just that: a letter to a historical church written by one who admired the church but was not its founder nor had ever been there. The Roman Christians knew of Paul and loved him from a distance. They had not been visited by an apostle, so far as we know, and greatly desired to see him and be blessed by him. Besides apostolic authority, Paul would supply them with powerful ammunition for persuading the unbelieving Jews and skeptical Gentiles. He was now in Corinth, just a short sail across the Adriatic, and boats were coming and going every day from the port on the inlet. He was farther west than he had been before. Surely he would continue just a little farther and visit them.

Paul assures them at the outset that it is not for lack of desire that he has not come to them—that in fact he longs to see them to impart some spiritual gift, has often purposed to do so, and prays that it will finally be possible. He is not intimidated by the great metropolis. The gospel of Christ has never shamed him. At the end of the epistle he will return to the question of why he has not visited them and will not presently do so. He is a pioneer missionary. They already have a flourishing church. He is persuaded they are "full of goodness, filled with all knowledge, able also to admonish one another" (Rom. 15:14). He will stop off in Rome on his way to Spain and refresh himself while they provision his journey west.

For now Paul will give them a masterful exposition of the gospel styled as a rebuttal of Jewish objections. The Roman believers are established in the rudimentary truths. But Paul will give them firepower for their testimony to the large Jewish population lately returned to Rome. I imagine that Paul is supplying them with a refined version of the synagogue sermons he has preached everywhere but Rome. Though they will not realize their desire to see him in person, they will not be denied this benefit granted the other churches.

I like to read the first four chapters of Romans as an enacted first encounter of a synagogue congregation with the gospel of Christ preached by the apostle Paul. In chapters 1 and 2 it assumes a mixed audience of Gentiles and Jews, common in synagogues. It stages Paul the disputer, anticipating hostile questions at key points.

> What advantage then hath the Jew? Or what profit is there of circumcision? (3:1)
> Do we then make void the law through faith? (3:31)
> What shall we say then? Shall we continue in sin, that grace may abound? (6:1)

I hear Paul parrying questions from sneering religionists, swaggering authorities on the law who will bully him if they can—as they did Jesus. Instead Paul, like his Master, brings their taunting questions into the service of his argument.

Paul, when meeting fierce opposition in the synagogue at Corinth, left it and took up his ministry in a house that "joined hard to the synagogue" (Acts 18:7); and Paul, by chapter 12 of Romans, is addressing believers about particular questions and issues. In the background of what he has to say about the covenants and election is the bristling mindset of Jewish national privilege. There is now a new spiritual Israel—a new flock, a new vine, a new racial Head, a new chosen group. Drama in the synagogue meets us in Romans 1 to 11. In my mind, at least, it does.

I don't have to insist on my mental staging of the argument in Romans to benefit from the experience. Paul's argument is audience sensitive. We find in it lives and life situations like our own, or that could be like our own were we so dedicated as were Paul and his associate believers. We can relate personally to what we read from these pages and richly gain.

In the last chapter, Paul greets his friends. Among them is "Rufus chosen in the Lord, and his mother and mine" (Rom. 16:13). To feed our thinking about Rufus, we can turn to Mark 15:21, where we are informed that Simon the Cyrenian had two sons named Alexander and Rufus, evidently well known to Mark's intended readers. *Simon*—unlike *Rufus* and *Alexander*—is a Jewish name. Cyrene was a Roman town in North Africa with a converted Jewish population. Tradition has it that Simon was a native African. A native African would have stood out in the crowd as an obvious foreigner. His selection for an ignominious role would not have inflamed the Jewish onlookers.

If so, it is fascinating to suppose—not entirely without evidence—that Simon of Cyrene was a Jewish convert who like the Ethiopian eunuch had come to worship in Jerusalem at Passover time. He found himself (to his mind) in the wrong place at the wrong time but because of his encounter with the Savior became a believer, returned home, and won his family to the Lord. His wife saw in Paul a man severed from his family and determined, as mothers do and as distance permitted, to take charge of his needs. The expression "chosen in the Lord" may suggest an extraordinary intervention in salvation and would resonate were this Rufus also Simon's son. Was his wife Paul's surrogate mother?

The last chapter of Romans contains another tantalizing detail easily passed over. Paul desires that his greeting be given to several of his kinsmen, two of whom "were in Christ before me" (16:7). Could this penetration of the gospel into his own family account partially for the ferocity of Saul's attack on the Jewish

Christians? Could it explain why a tenderhearted mother would adopt an estranged Paul as a third son?

I can't be sure. But reflecting on these *perhapses* vitalized my readerly encounter with the Paul of Romans.

> *Thoughtful reading also reflects on the setting of an entire book.*

3
CONSIDER THE
AUDIENCE

The Epistle to the Philippians is for many Christians the most personally affecting of the prison epistles of Paul. It addresses a congregation rich in the Christian graces and passionate in their love for the apostle who first encountered them not in a synagogue but on the banks of a river at an hour of prayer.

Paul was under house arrest in Rome when he was writing his letter to the Philippian church. He is loved by the church, and he loves them. He has little fault to find with them. He reminds them of some cautions he has given them before and exhorts them to continue in the Lord. But what pervades the letter is his gratitude for their response to his ministry. He longs for them as much as they long for him. His yearning for them and theirs for him are everywhere apparent. "God is my record, how greatly I long after you all in the bowels of Jesus Christ" (Phil. 1:8).

Paul is sure he will see them again (2:24), but in the meantime while he is away from them in prison, they will be enabled by God. He has given them already what they need for their spiritual growth, though he looks forward to returning "for your furtherance and joy of faith" (1:25).

This brings us to chapter 2 and the passage in question. Paul, as so often elsewhere in his writings, enjoins the believers to unite in humility and love, to be "of one mind" (2:2) toward one another. To that end he sets before them the example of Christ—"Let this mind be in you, which was also in Christ Jesus" (2:5)—connecting it with what has been troubling their minds. What has been troubling their minds is how they will get along without him.

Paul assures the Philippians that their church can go forward without his physical presence, without his looking over their shoulders. With his instructions and his example (3:17) and their vigilance, the church will survive and prosper as before. They need to obey as before what he has told them. They must take on their own oversight with what they have seen of his care and concern. He couches his admonition in puzzling words.

> Wherefore, my beloved, as ye have always obeyed, not as in
> my presence only, but now much more in my absence, work
> out your own salvation with fear and trembling. (Phil. 2:12)

Work out your own salvation? How can this injunction square with what we have learned of salvation from Paul's other writings?

> For by grace are ye saved through faith; and that not of
> yourselves: it is the gift of God: not of works, lest any man
> should boast. (Eph. 2:8–9)

Paul has thundered in Romans and Galatians against the great fraud of rabbinical Judaism on this point, the trust in meritorious works. How can he here contradict this great gospel truth that has been at the core of his preaching and contending for these years? *Work out your own salvation?*

Paul earlier in the epistle reports he is confident that God's enabling his witness in the Roman court "shall turn to my salvation through your prayer" (Phil. 1:19). That should remind us that the word *salvation* in the Bible has a wide semantic range. Broadly it means "deliverance." Clearly Paul here means by *salvation* his deliverance from imprisonment, not from eternal punishment. He is sure he will be freed to continue his work. Meanwhile they should consider themselves prepared to go on without him in the work he, Paul, has begun.

Though they will be without Paul, they will not be without Paul's God. His God will continue to be, as He has till then, "work[ing] in you both to will and to do of his good pleasure" (2:13).

Paul had struck this note at the outset, addressing their concern that what he had put into them will fade. He prays for them with joy, "being confident of this very thing, that he which hath begun a good work in you [he has colabored with God] will perform it until the day of Jesus Christ" (1:6). God's ongoing ministry in the present epistle is evidence. It will last.

But we are not through with this thought line. Or rather it is not through with us.

In chapter 3 Paul uses himself as an example of what they can do while he is away from them. He is dismissive of his gifts and past accomplishments. His pressing interests are those ahead. His life is a race for a prize. Its goal is perfection, a fully achieved life in the plan of God. His heart's desire is that

> I may know him, and the power of his resurrection, and the fellowship of his sufferings, being made conformable unto his death; if by any means I might attain unto the resurrection of the dead. Not as though I had already attained, either were already perfect: but I follow after, if that I may apprehend [seize upon, grasp] that for which also I am apprehended of Christ Jesus. . . . I press toward the mark for the prize of the high calling of God in Christ Jesus. (Phil. 3:10–12, 14)

Paul says his beloved Philippians should be doing this also. "Brethren, be followers together of me, and mark them which walk so as ye have us for an ensample" (v. 17). Notice that the race is here identified as a walk. Distance walking is an Olympic contest, and a grueling one.

Paul's account of his striving in this passage may revive the earlier question about his confidence in his salvation. Paul is exerting himself to the fullest "if by any means I might attain unto the resurrection of the dead" (v. 11). Once again, are we to think Paul may be in doubt about his salvation? Is his part in that final resurrection of the redeemed only a hope, a wish?

In Romans 6 and elsewhere Paul speaks of a resurrection that is even now taking place. It is not just analogous with the historical resurrection of the Savior; it is derivative from it and enabled by it, and it continues on.

> Know ye not, that so many of us as were baptized into Jesus Christ were baptized into his death? Therefore we are buried with him by baptism into death [baptism in the early church followed quickly upon conversion so the two could be spoken of together]: that like as Christ was raised up from the dead by the glory of the Father, even so we also should walk in newness of life. For if we have been planted together in the likeness of his death, we shall be also in the likeness of his resurrection: knowing this, that our old man is crucified with him, that the body of sin might be destroyed, that henceforth we should not serve sin. . . . Likewise reckon ye also yourselves to be dead indeed unto sin, but alive unto God through Jesus Christ our Lord. (Rom. 6:3–6, 11)

The connection of saving belief with the death and resurrection of Christ shoots through Paul's writings.

> I am crucified with Christ: nevertheless I live; yet not I, but Christ liveth in me: and the life which I now live in the flesh I live by the faith of the Son of God, who loved me, and gave himself for me. (Gal. 2:20; see also Col. 2:12–14; 3:1)

Paul echoes the Savior's words recorded in John 12:24 on the need of a seed to fall into the ground and die in order to grow. The resurrection spoken of in Philippians 3 is to a fully formed life in the image of its Creator.

If we read around our passage in Philippians 3, fore and aft, it can appear less startling than before. Paul's zeal as a brilliant young Pharisee and his blameless life "touching the righteousness which is in the law" (v. 6) did not count toward his salvation. He will relegate it to the trash heap so that "I may win Christ, and be found in him, not having mine own righteousness, which is of the law, but that which is through the faith of Christ, the righteousness which is of God by faith" (v. 8–9). What goads him onward now is a compelling desire to "know him, and the power of his resurrection, and the fellowship of his sufferings, being made conformable unto his death" (v. 10).

Paul sets himself before the Philippians as an example (v. 17) but, lest he be misunderstood, stresses they should not think of him as having already arrived at his destination in his spiritual journey. They should not regard him "as though I had already attained, either were already perfect" (v. 12). Instead, he is pressing toward that goal. "I follow after, if that I may apprehend that for which also I am apprehended of Christ Jesus" (v. 12). Paul is striving to take possession of what he is already possessed of by virtue of his being possessed by Christ. He desires to actualize to the fullest in this life, in so far as he is able, what is guaranteed him in the life to come.

The consummation of a work underway in a believer is what is being designated as a hoped resurrection. To put it inadequately, Paul would minimize the culture shock incumbent in the passage from this life to the next. He will not be among the number of those saved just by fire.

We have followed the thought narratives of two epistles of Paul addressing the desire of congregations to connect with a distant spiritual leader. A takeaway for this reader is what should be the ultimate goal of all leadership, to render its presence unnecessary.[1] Paul encouraged the Philippians they could now go on without him, with his example and the examples of others like him, obeying what he had told them. The congregation at Rome likewise could continue to thrive in the absence of Paul, for that assembly, like the Philippian church, had begun without him and was doing well by itself. As the need arose, he would boost and correct both congregations by letter.

Overarching all would be the great example of our Lord who Himself had comforted His anxious disciples that last dark night with the same thought (John 14). The eleven would thrive after His departure with what had been provided for them—a Comforter who would be not only *with* them but also *in* them.

---

1. The author had intended to expand on this concept within this book, but in a providential irony, he passed from this life to the next before penning those words. He, himself, was rendered unnecessary, his life's work complete.

He Himself would be with them too, though not visibly, as the stock of their true vine (John 15:1).

Thoughtful reading with sensitivity to audience can have a bearing on interpretation.

4

LISTEN TO SCRIPTURE

How easy it is to come to Scripture with blinders on, the blinders of what we want to do with it and find in it for our own purposes. We start before we should in a passage and stop before we should and edit in the middle where we shouldn't and misconstrue what's left from our editing. We continue on our way speaking to Scripture rather than allowing Scripture to speak to us.

To discover meaning in a piece of writing other than the meaning you want to find there entails reading with receptive, even a sort of passive, alertness. With all the faculties attentive and with an openness to multiple contexts, you take an impression, test it, refine it, relate it, and perhaps store it for the time being. The process is cumulative and critical. It need not require a slower, more deliberate pace than the usual. Our speed increases with reading of high interest. The French mathematician Blaise Pascal wrote, "When we read too fast or too slowly, we understand nothing."[1] The process described here does require a state of mind. But that state of mind is the natural way we read what excites us. When we delight in what we read, we truly read.

---

1. Blaise Pascal, Roger Ariew. *Pensées.* (Indianapolis: Hackett Publishing Company, Inc., 2004), 12.

One can be impressed as I have been with the fact of three female personages in the book of Proverbs. Two are set in parallel relationship. Whereas both the strange woman and Wisdom are in the business of alluring young men to accept offers of love, the one entices privately at night, the other publicly in the day. The master of the house is absent and would be disapproving of the nocturnal solicitation in the one case, but ever-present, by implication, and delighting in the activity of his child in the other.

There is a third woman in Proverbs 31 who has spoken no doubt often and to good purpose whose words are not given. I imagine that the celebration of the good wife is meant to climax a series of female exemplars. Her description read closely and unforced is a concretization of what is being solicited in the call of the allegorical Wisdom. Her gracious, purposive energies outmatch the wily sinuous overtures of the strange woman. She provides a flesh-and-blood instance of what is being promised to the young man of Proverbs, presumably of near marriageable age, by divine Wisdom, which will be particularized in chapters leading up to it.

It is natural and divinely meant for youth to dream. Youth will be dreaming, nurturing desires and hopes, and picturing them. Their dreams are of great importance. Dreams will determine what they become. How to get them dreaming in the right direction—that is a parent's great challenge. The compiler of Proverbs took up the challenge. Chapter 31 is not just an addendum. It supplies a worthy fantasy for a youth approaching manhood, one toward which what we may call the story line of this Book of Wisdom drives—a description of a virtuous woman, a wife and mother worthy of praise. Dream that way, not the other way, my son. Choose love, not anti-love its masquerade.

A bird's-eye view of a passage or a book of Scripture need not be insensitive to pertinent detail. It is reported that an eagle perched on the roof of a ten-story building can see an ant crawling on the sidewalk.[2] We may notice that the good wife cares about the particulars of her husband's appearance. He occupies a place of distinction at the city gate, and she makes sure he is dressed for it. She also cares about her own appearance. She wants her family to be pleased with her total person. She travels far to supply her family's needs, and then some. She can work into the night to finish a task. She keeps up her house.

My account of an idea thread in Proverbs came to me unsolicited from reading with passive alertness and imaginative extensions. I would not insist upon its full accuracy.

I absolutely concur with what a learned Renaissance scholar said about subjectivity in interpretation. "What kills good poems through the eye is a reader's blind determination to see nothing in the round world but himself, and the wish to read without attending to what the author could have in mind is one form of it."[3]

We mustn't confuse meaning with significance. But a total responsiveness to sections of Scripture has supplied me with thoughts serving my spiritual growth and elevating my delight in the God of the Word of God.

Thoughtful reading allows Scripture
to speak to us.

---

2. "What If Humans Had Eagle Vision," LiveScience (website); Future US Inc; Feb. 24, 2012, https://www.livescience.com/18658-humans-eagle-vision.html.
3. Rosemond Tuve, *A Reading of George Herbert* (Chicago: University of Chicago Press, 1952), 109.

5

MOTIVATE THE MIND

Let's read for pleasure and profit a story from the Old Testament books of Israel's history, that fly-over territory so easily skipped or skimmed. Notice that a narrative of Scripture can carry a good deal of conceptual weight. The conceptual load it carries can inform and motivate the mind.

GARRISON

There was a lot of sneaking going on that night around Saul's home in Gibeah. Saul had slunk back home from his encampment in Gilgal, the original staging area of Israel's army under Joshua by the Jordan a few miles from Jericho. Saul with his three thousand chosen troops were to wait for Samuel to come and deliver the blessing of the Lord on his kingdom and the present military operation. Saul jumped ahead and conducted a sacrifice himself and lost the blessing of God on his rule. Saul sneaked back to Gibeah and had set up court somewhere out of view under a pomegranate tree. It was night (1 Sam. 14).

Jonathan was about to do some sneaking of his own. He had created the problem, attacking a Philistine garrison, arousing the Philistines who had bullied Israel and were now poised to wipe them out. They had been sneaking in, had flooded the zone with an incredible number of chariots, a vast cavalry, and uncountable foot soldiers. Saul's chosen fighters had reduced to six hundred (v. 2). The rest had sneaked away to their homes if not joined their fellow Benjamites in thickets and caves.

Now it is night, and we have a secret conversation between Jonathan and his armor bearer. He had earlier been left at Gibeah with a thousand troops to defend the town. Jonathan floats a notion.

> Come, and let us go over unto the garrison of these un-
> circumcised: it may be that the Lord will work for us: for
> there is no restraint to the Lord to save by many or by few.
> (1 Sam. 14: 6)

Consider the parts of what Jonathan said. "It *may be* that the Lord will work for us." Jonathan's proposal is without *presumption of its success.* "For there is no restraint to the Lord to save by many or by few." Jonathan's proposal however is not without confidence in the *possibility of its success.* This is quintessential faith—assurance without presumption.

Faith is validated by action. The armor bearer's response is priceless.

> Do all that is in thine heart: turn thee; behold, I am with
> thee according to thy heart. (1 Sam. 14:7)

In my paraphrase: "Let's roll!"

And they crawl up the face of the rock on hands and knees to the flat place and begin chopping down the guard, Jonathan striking and the armor bearer finishing. They had got only twenty before God sent a mighty earthquake that put the Philistine army in mad flight.

This incident, the first recorded episode in Saul's reign, brings to mind another first incident in the Gospels. When Jesus descended from the mountain in Matthew 8, a leper came to Him with a simple request couched as a statement.

> Lord, if thou wilt, thou canst make me clean. (Matt. 8:2)

Here again is assurance without presumption. Jesus replied "I will" (v. 3). He touched the scabrous flesh of the helpless man and made him whole. He became Himself unclean to make the leper clean. It was a response by the Lord to quintessential faith. A lesson we can take away from the examples of the armor bearer and the leper is the appeal to God of simple faith. It moves Him to move, not that He is otherwise resistant.

Let's consider now the location of Jonathan's victory of faith. Conquering armies have learned it is easier to conquer territory than to hold it. Neither was easy for the Carthaginian military leader Hannibal, who crossed the Alps into Italy with a number of war elephants and a depleted but powerful army. He joined with anti-Roman forces at the foot of the Pyrenees and ravaged Italy for two years. But he couldn't occupy the territory he had won. He was eventually forced to retreat to Carthage (now known as Tunisia).

The Philistines found the same to be true when Jonathan and his armor bearer attacked their garrison at Michmash, deep in Israel's territory. When David had established his kingdom (2 Samuel 8), he placed garrisons in the bordering nations, to the north in Syria and to the south in Edom. He had natural boundaries to the east with the Jordan River and to the west with the Mediterranean Sea, though he chose not to drive the Philistines into the sea. He would keep the Philistines intimidated. To this end he had the help of his personal guard led by Benaiah, a superb warrior from the southerly region of the Philistine coastal strip at odds with King Achish of Gath. Benaiah had joined David's band of followers when he was in flight from Saul.

Both the Philistine garrison and David's served a common purpose. A garrison is a fortified military outpost, staffed with a select guard. It is intended to keep the enemy out of conquered territory. It has a defensive mission, but one which may become quickly an offensive one. A garrison needs determined troops and alert sentries. Jesus tells a parable in Luke 19 of a nobleman taking a journey who left his lands under the supervision of his servants. Since his people hated him, his servants had a real challenge to carry out. He told them, "Occupy till I come" (v. 13). They were to maintain his rule and serve his interests in what amounted to enemy territory.

We too live in enemy territory. That territory is without but also, and especially, within. We need God to mount a guard over us—a garrison. That He does so is made clear in this comforting passage.

> Be careful for nothing; but in every thing by prayer and
> supplication with thanksgiving let your requests be made
> known unto God. And the peace of God, which passeth all
> understanding, shall keep your hearts and minds through
> Christ Jesus. (Phil. 4:6–7)

This passage is often incorporated in benedictions with a slight alteration in wording.

> May the peace of God, which passeth all understanding,
> garrison your hearts and minds through Christ Jesus.

The word *garrison* here is more exactly reflective of the original Greek than the KJV *keep*. Here is the *Zondervan KJV Study Bible* note on it.

> A military concept depicting a sentry standing guard. God's
> protective custody of those who are in Christ Jesus extends
> to the core of their beings and to their deepest intentions.[1]

We too have boundary work to do, and God has prepared us for it. We must be strong and alert. We must apply our resources. We war against foreign foes—"against principalities, against powers, against the rulers of the darkness of this world, against spiritual wickedness in high places" (Eph. 6:12). We also stand guard against home threats, the enemy within us, the assault of our disabling fears and desires.

God can help us garrison the boundaries and firm the battle lines. Are we attending to contested territories within and without, keeping up our defenses in areas of past defeat, even advancing our battle stations against enemy lines?

These thoughts have come to me from a readerly reading of a fascinating story.

What follows is another story, equal I think in interest and in idea payload, from a New Testament history book. The story begins with the concept of waking in Isaiah 51, which leads us to the gate.

---

1. *Zondervan KJV Study Bible* (Grand Rapids: Zondervan, 1995), 1712.

THE IRON GATE

Isaiah 51 and onward is one of the most magnificent sections of Scripture, and I have so many times gotten caught up in it. Israel is being wakened by Jehovah from her sleep. Her enemies are gone. Her captivity is over. I'll share my thought stream as I read this passage and then the passage it led to.

"Awake, awake, put on strength," comes the call in Isaiah 51:9. "Awake, awake, stand up," comes the call in verse 17 to a people who have "drunk at the hand of the LORD the cup of his fury," drunk "the dregs of the cup of trembling, and wrung them out," squeezed out the last drops from the settlings at the bottom of the cup, and are in a drunkard's deep sleep. "Awake, awake; put on thy strength, O Zion," comes the renewed call in chapter 52, verse 1 but with additions. "Shake thyself from the dust; arise, and sit down, O Jerusalem: loose thyself from the bands of thy neck, O captive daughter of Zion" (v. 2). Israel must be roused from her stupor and freed from her bonds. Her rebellion against Jehovah has brought her low. He will now release her, lift her, beautify her.

I think of that great chapter just following that begins, "Ho, every one that thirsteth, come ye to the waters, and he that hath no money; come ye, buy, and eat; yea, come, buy wine and milk without money and without price" (55:1), and goes on,

> Let the wicked forsake his way, and the unrighteous man his thoughts; and let him return unto the LORD, and he will have mercy upon him; and to our God, for he will abundantly pardon. For my thoughts are not your thoughts, neither are your ways my ways, saith the LORD. For as the heavens are higher than the earth, so are my ways higher than your ways, and my thoughts than your thoughts. (Isa. 55:7–9)

Be aware that the Hebrew word translated *thoughts* is not referring to a higher knowledge (that is evident from the context) but means instead *intentions*, as it does elsewhere in the Hebrew Scriptures. God is saying, "I have higher purposes toward you than you have had and have toward Me." These are the words of a grieving, longsuffering God, what G. Campbell Morgan in his commentary on Jeremiah called "the challenge of wounded love."[2]

What God says He is going to do will be a spiritual as well as physical deliverance from captivity. In Ezekiel He likens it to exchanging a heart of flesh for a heart of stone. This section of Isaiah brought to my mind these passages in the other two Major Prophets. But what sent my mind on a journey were the physical details of the passage, which brought to mind an event in Acts. *Wake up, Peter. Get up, stand up, put on your garment (not here your beautiful garments), and follow me.* His chains fall off, and then the exit. I'm referring of course to the fascinating story Luke tells with such enlivening detail in Acts 12 about Peter and the angel, to which we now turn.

Herod is riding high. He has killed John's brother James "with the sword" (Acts 12:2) to please the Jews. Peter is in prison "delivered him to four quaternions of soldiers to keep him" (v. 4), awaiting no doubt a similar fate, but Herod has delayed it till Easter (Luke's Gentile name for the Feast of Unleavened Bread) so he can get the most value from it from the Jews assembled for Passover. Peter must have had in his mind the Lord's words about his death in John 21. The church was praying. Notice the detail in the account of what follows.

> The same night Peter was sleeping between two soldiers, bound with two chains: and the keepers before the door kept the prison. And, behold, the angel of the Lord came upon him, and a light shined in the prison: and he smote Peter on the side, and raised him up, saying, Arise up quickly. And his chains fell off from his hands. And the angel said unto him, Gird thyself, and bind on thy sandals. And so he did. (Acts 12:6–8)

Peter is in prison asleep. He is chained between two guards. A light shines in the prison. He is thumped on the side. He is raised up and told to get up! The chains fall from his hands. Now he can dress himself. How characteristic of Scripture to blend the human

---

2. G. Campbell Morgan. *Studies in the Prophecy of Jeremiah.* (Grand Rapids: Fleming H. Revell, Co., 1955), 35.

and divine. God did what Peter *could not do* and then told Peter what *to do*. "And so he did" (v. 8). There was co-agency in Peter's deliverance. He had to obey his instructions, "and so he did." Do you need God to get you out of a tight place? He may have some instructions for you. You may have a part in it. Better listen up.

Peter does. More commands. "Cast thy garment about thee [again notice Peter's part], and follow me" (v. 8). Peter had heard these words before—once by a river and twice by a lake. The Christian life with its challenges and beckonings and disappointments, its hopes fulfilled and hopes dashed, is all about "follow me." Peter as before obeyed. "And he went out, and followed him" (v. 9).

Peter was not done yet. God's work is to open doors. Peter's work was to follow. There was that last door.

> When they were past the first and the second ward [guard],
> they came unto the iron gate that leadeth unto the city;
> which opened to them of his own accord: and they went
> out, and passed on through one street; and forthwith the
> angel departed from him. (Acts 12:10)

That iron gate, the last one, is the one that leads to the city, to the freedom of a fulfilled life. Now my thoughts are being carried to those iron gates that stand in the path of God's best for us. How do you unlock a locked up mind? Is there anything more daunting than sullen mindlock, than wounded mindlock?

I've been meditating on that question for years. A husband wonders about that. His wife may also—about that fortified prison yard of angers and hurts that cannot be discussed and walls out their happiness. Good parents who desire the best for their child are perplexed by it. The iron gate. What can swing it open? What can free up a stiffened troubled mind?

It must unlock from within. But can it do so without help? The captive self—chained by vain fantasies and false fears—will, like Peter, have to awake, arise, stand, reclothe, and follow his Guide through the door he has closed.

Thoughtful reading carries conceptual weight.

PART 2

FOLLOWING THE STORY

We should engage in reading that invites Scripture to reach the receptive mind with its own agenda, an agenda of which the mind may very well be unaware.

In what follows we read a lengthy section of Scripture that tells Elijah's story. We will read of events and interactions; we will read with curiosity, imagination, and openness. We will allow Scripture to tell us his story.

A readerly approach to Scripture can produce fresh insights, bringing a long stretch of narrative to life.

6

ELIJAH'S FIRST CONFRONTATION

THE BUILDUP

David and his son Solomon each ruled Israel for forty years. They ruled either directly or by vassal states a territory stretching from the Gulf of Aqaba, the tip of the eastern fork of the Red Sea, well beyond Damascus in modern Syria. Solomon solidified his father's territorial gains and extended his political control as far as the headwaters of the Euphrates in the Lebanon Mountains. It was the high point of Israel's political power and grandeur.

Spiritually it was another story. In the later years of Solomon's reign, his many wives turned his heart to idolatry, and the religious tone of the nation began disintegrating. Trouble in the ruler means trouble in the state, and under Solomon Israel spiritually began her long decline. Solomon's disregard for God's stipulations forbidding marriage to foreigners appears in the fact that Rehoboam, his royal heir, was the son of an Ammonite woman. The Ammonites and the Moabites to their south were descendants of Lot, nephew to Abraham; and because of this family connection, Israel was forbidden to destroy them. They inhabited the land east of the Jordan River below the territory assigned to Reuben. They had vile, cruel gods.

Political cohesion under Solomon had become delicate when the throne passed to his son. His subjects resented their enforced labor for Solomon's building projects. When their tribal leaders asked him for relief from his father's severity, Rehoboam answered them with threats. It was a foolish response. The ten northern tribes rejected his rule and the royal line of Judah. They formed their own nation under the leadership of Jeroboam, who had been a thorn in Solomon's side. Israel would no longer be the original nation of twelve tribes. The northern tribes kept the name Israel and were adversaries of Judah to the south.

To keep the northern kingdom intact, Jeroboam instituted a new religious practice, a pretense of Jehovah worship that revived the calf worship instigated by Aaron while Moses was on the mount receiving the covenant from God. He built altars for the calves at either end of the tribal territory, Bethel at the south and Dan to the north, and created his own priesthood from the lowest of the people, the riffraff of society (those without a job?). The writer of 1 Kings obviously regards this manmade religious arrangement as a monstrosity. Jeroboam's name lives in infamy in Old Testament history as the founder of a defiant nation and a defiant religion. Idolatry maintained its hold on its worshipers through the accompanying sensual practices. Israel was forbidden to plant a grove near an altar to God (Deut. 16:21).

The sins of Jeroboam were continued by his son Nadab, the assassin Baasha, his son Elah, the assassin Zimri, and his conqueror Omri, founder of the city Samaria and the wickedest line in Israel's history. Omri, like Jeroboam, reigned for twenty-two years but did worse than all that were before him, provoking God to anger with the idolatrous worship inaugurated by its founder (1 Kings 16:25).

But then came his son, Ahab, who outdid his father in vile worship. He married a Phoenician princess, who set out to transform the religion of Israel from the ground up. She replaced calf worship with the worship of the god of her people, Baal, and dispensed with all pretense of Jehovah recognition. Israel would have a new *Lord God*. Baal was a storm deity, a god of lightning and fire, a hurler of thunderbolts like the Greek god Zeus, and the sender of rain for the crops. Jezebel's father was Ethbaal, ruler of the Sidonians (v. 31). According to the Jewish historian Josephus, Ethbaal ruled both Sidon and Tyre for thirty-four years.

Whereas Jeroboam had relocated the center of religion from Jerusalem in the south to northern Israel with the calf altars at Bethel and Dan, Jezebel would turn religion further to the north, making Baal worship, the religion of her homeland with its cruelty and sensuality and perversion, the religion of her new land.

Now we have set the scene for a great story. It will resonate at every point with the history of the preceding chapters, which I have summarized. Israel's covenant with God has been rejected. Her religion is corrupt. Her rule is up for grabs. Her morality is in steep descent. It would seem that those faithful to the true God who have not been destroyed by Jezebel might as well give up hope.

CONFRONTATION AND PROCLAMATION

A figure appears suddenly out of nowhere. We don't know his parentage. We don't know exactly where he came from. We know where Gilead is, in the tribal territory across Jordan to the north. But where was Tishbe? Parentage and location are key facts in biblical identification, but family descent and patrimony are not indicated here, so evidently neither is what is important about him. His importance consists in the declaration he has come to deliver to the king of Israel. It will set the king back on his heels.

You like drama? Here is a face-off like few you will ever read. Have you had "out-of-nowheres" in your life? Have they been mostly bad? Mostly good? Which get remembered the most? Is your God the God of both good and bad?

Notice how Elijah identifies himself. His identity consists of his official function. His personal background is of no consequence. His personal thoughts are not to the point. What he has to say has been delivered to him. It is his words, but his words are the utterance of that great one whom he waits on in readiness—"before whom I stand" (1 Kings 18:15).

We will see this occur again in 2 Corinthians 5:20 where Paul identifies himself similarly in terms of his divinely appointed role. He is an ambassador sent from the court of God with a role assigned him, a portfolio for introduction, and a message to deliver. The message can be stated concisely. It contains a welcome and a warning. Though winsome, it is heavy with consequences.

Elijah's message begins with an oath formula that is not just an oath formula: "As the Lord God of Israel liveth" (1 Kings 17:1). It voices the great theme of Elijah's ministry and of the chapters in 1 and 2 Kings devoted to it. Elijah has crossed Jordan from the east with a declaration from the Lord God of Israel who still lives as Israel's God. He has not been banished by the new territorial god of Jezebel. Baal's territory has not spread south. That's only Jezebel and Ahab's wishful thinking. Jehovah still rules both east and west of Jordan. He rules not only Judah, still officially faithful to His worship, but also the ten breakaway tribes to the north.

We will notice the prominence of references to *the Lord God, the word of the Lord, the Lord my God, the Lord thy God,* as well as to the lowercase *lord* referring to an earthly master. What I call the *lordness* theme is the main thread of the story in these chapters. Perhaps it can be considered the main thread in both a believer's life as well as an unbeliever's as God reads lives. We see both such lives—believers and unbelievers—in our story.

Elijah's message strikes at the heart of the Sidonians' claims for Baal. Baal, as noted earlier, was a vegetation deity responsible for sending the seasonal rains. He brought saving moisture from the Great Sea to the west. Elijah, emissary from the court of Israel's true God, says there will be no rain till he says so—that is, until he reappears with words from Israel's God to that effect. Baal is being tested. Poor Baal. Baal worship is being exposed. Poor religion. Baal worshipers are being shown the futility of their worship. Poor worshipers. Will they continue in their worship after it proves useless? Of course, because of what accompanies it, the addictive sensuality.

Elijah is so closely identified with his Lord's message that he can speak of his Lord's word as "my word" (1 Kings 17:1).

Notice the simplicity of Elijah's mind world, or what is revealed of it to us. Devotion to God tends to simplify the Christian psyche. It tends to reduce conflicts, fears, competing inclinations, much of life's push and pull. Stresses and strains are inevitable in a fallen world containing fallen people. Paul noted that complications increase with married life, explaining why for his calling it was better he stay unmarried. But whatever one's life state, a firm spiritual center simplifies the life. When obedience to God becomes a no-brainer, many troubling life questions fall away or fail to appear.

THE RETURN

Now the word of the Lord comes to His emissary and has to do with His emissary's personal need. God's people suffer during His judgment of unbelief, but they are always in His mind. Here God must preserve His instrument for the role to which he has been called. But also God cares for him as a person on his own account—an important fact.

God's command comes to Elijah with the same emphatic force with which it came through Elijah to Ahab. "Get thee hence" (v. 3). God separates Elijah from the abhorred land and primary area of judgment. The drought will reach beyond Ahab's kingdom, but for now there is a spring running into Jordan from the east. Elijah is to hide himself. It is all right to hide if God tells you to hide. He can preserve you in hiding or out of hiding. Israel was no place for a visible, vocal prophet at that time. It did not deserve or need an elaboration of Elijah's message.

God again has commanded, this time about the means of Elijah's sustenance. He has water. He will have food. It will be more than adequate—bread and flesh, what we call meat. It will come with regularity, morning and evening, from someone's kitchen or buffet. From the royal table? Wouldn't that be an irony! The carriers are carrions. Ravens were unclean birds according to the Mosaic law. Israel was spiritually unclean. Better to eat from unclean birds than to eat in an unclean land.

Notice the emphasis on Elijah's obedience to a divine command. "So he went and did according unto the word of the Lord: for he went and dwelt [stayed] by the brook" (v. 5). The detail seems gratuitous until we understand its importance for the emphasis of the story. Elijah's behavior is modeling the simple, direct obedience to Israel's God that Israel has denied Him.

Then comes a surprise to the reader as perhaps also to Elijah: the brook dries up. Did the ravens too stop coming? Sometimes what God gives with one hand He takes away with the other. "The Lord gave, and the Lord hath taken away," Job said (Job 1:21). This unpredictability of God's ways can occur in His dealings with us both small and large. We'll see more of that later.

But the story does not end there. It never ends there. God, our provider, never leaves us destitute.

NORTH TO SIDON

God has more than one means of providing for Elijah, and for us. The brook has dried up. Presumably the ravens have stopped coming. Maybe supplies ran out for the buffet or the kitchen. The drought was severe. The true Lord of Israel gives Elijah a new command. Get up and go north into Baal country, into the heart of Jezebel's land, ruled by her father, Ethbaal (1 Kings 17:9).

Baal has been brought into Israel, God's land, from the north. Baal has displaced Jehovah in the minds of the people and their rulers as the Lord of Israel. Now the true God of Israel in a counterthrust is penetrating Baal's territory. Granted it is seemingly on a small scale, but Israel's God measures His actions differently from the way we sometimes do.

THE WIDOW

God tells Elijah He has commanded a widow of Zarephath (Greek *Sarepta* in Luke 4:26) to sustain him (1 Kings 17:9). He has been sustained by the mineral kingdom, the brook, in conjunction with the animal kingdom, the ravens. These natural means are not just natural causation. They have behind them the supernatural, God's attention and purposes and His commands. Now Elijah's provision will be taken further up the scale of creation. He will be sustained by human means.

There will be an interaction between persons with initial resistance on the part of the widow recorded in her conversation with Elijah. We have no record of a conversation between God and the ravens. Animals are governed by instinct, though God can drive them against their instinct as with the ravens. Maybe there was a bit of hesitation before the birds refrained from consuming those morsels. Maybe they weren't decomposed enough!

Humans are more complicated. They have wills, as we see from the woman's words to Elijah. Elijah exemplifies immediate unquestioning obedience. The widow hesitates, though she had received a prior command from God. But God through Elijah persists. Notice the stark contrast between Jehovah's detailed attention to three individuals in need and the cruel indifference and absolute impotence of the Sidonian god as he was conceived by his worshipers.

We have a wonderful story of contrasts. It takes us into the psychology of obedience, of the sort God expects, and of His tender patience in eliciting it. The widow "went and did according to the saying of Elijah" (v. 15). Her response is an example to us all. Notice what it involved. "Fear not; go and do as thou hast said: but make me thereof a little cake *first*, and bring it unto me, and *after* make for thee and for thy son" (v. 13).

Do we have a life rule here? God made the business difficult for the woman. There was *complication* there. Understand that she was caught between two very reasonable and natural impulses—her love for her son and her duty to Elijah and his God.

There was *contingency*. She had to begin with the Lord's part before receiving her part. We all need to keep a check on the *firstness* and *afterness* of our spiritual lives. Here we have the true order. The order can get reversed. God can be given the leftovers. If so, He'll return to us His leftovers, and they won't be as good as what the ravens brought Elijah. The drought can overtake us along with God's enemies. If it does, it will be the best thing that can happen to us in our poor spiritual state.

I love the particulars of the story. The widow met Elijah by the gate of the city. Our God is a God of exquisite timing. She was gathering a couple of sticks to make a fire to cook a little piece of cornbread (!) to divide with her son. Elijah hadn't come. But then he pops up, just as he had earlier with Ahab. And God's remedy gets in motion. Notice the smallness. Just a pitcher of flour and a jar of oil. Remember the five loaves and two small fish of the little boy's lunch in Matthew 14? God likes to make much of little.

We learn a lot about God in this incident. Notice how the miracle expands. The meal and oil will supply not just the three of them but her entire household. They no doubt came flocking. God is not a miserly provisioner but a God of abundance. "I am come that they might have life, and . . . have it more abundantly" (John 10:10).

THE WIDOW'S SON

But the story doesn't end there. Partway through the three-year drought, God took the widow's son. It was another out-of-nowhere. Notice the parallel with the earlier experience. The brook and the ravens sustained Elijah, but after a while the brook dried up.

But deprivation was not the end of the story then nor would it be now. God had prepared sustenance for Elijah after the brook dried up, and it would be more agreeable even than that before. God would save him from starvation by an obedient widow and the widow and her son as well. He joined the household he had delivered as God's instrument and benefited from the deliverance himself.

Yet then events turned in reverse. Once again it appeared that what God had given with one hand He took away with the other. She was destitute again. Her son "fell sick," so sick "there was no breath left in him" (1 Kings 17:17). Devastated, the widow turned on Elijah: "What have I to do with thee, O thou man of God?" (v. 18). Israel's God and His prophet had raised her joy in order to mock it.

She over-interpreted the cause. Her thoughts went directly to her sin: "Art thou come unto me to call my sin to remembrance, and to slay my son?" (v. 18). Her thoughts went indirectly by implication to Elijah's God. Was Elijah's coming to Zarepheth only an apparent good? Was the miraculous provision in the drought only staging for this crushing blow? Had God replaced the three-year famine of the land with an endless drought of her soul? Are Jehovah's worshipers only His playthings?

We must be careful not to read too much into the widow woman's response. She was emptied out by her grief and in her disappointment spoke in anger. The incident is psychologically true. We can be too quick to draw conclusions about wild words at a time like this. Elijah did not dip into theology or the consolations of Scripture to respond to her. He knew what *not* to say.

And yet he also knew what *to* say. "Give me thy son" (v. 19). Those four words alone justify all the time we have spent with Elijah. I've never heard anything quite like this response of Elijah to the distraught widow's question in grief therapy. God is jealous of His authority in the deep valleys as well as on the hills and mountains of our lives in this fallen world,[1] wrote Handley Moule. We can count on God to know what He is doing. We can be sure He cares as much about what we care deeply about as we do—what is worthy of our care. Our precious things are precious to Him as well.

---

1. Handley Moule, *Thoughts for the Sundays of the Year* (Chattanooga, TN: AMG Publishers, 1997), 139.

Notice how the Lord spoke to the nobleman's dead daughter as He lifted her from her bed: *"Talitha Cumi;* [Little Lamb] . . . I say unto thee, arise"* (Mark 5:41). He cared for the child given Him by her father as His own. It can be consoling to have responded in the affirmative to the words of God from Elijah when one's own child is in view, "Give me thy child."

What happened then is most interesting. Elijah took the boy, who had stopped breathing, up to his chamber, his guest room. What was to take place there would be in private. There would be no sensationalism, just as when the Lord, in raising the nobleman's daughter, put all the mourners out of the room, allowing them to think later if they wished to that the girl had not really died.

Now it was Elijah's turn to question God. "And he cried unto the Lord, and said, O Lord my God [these words resonate in the ongoing question of Israel's true God, His goodness and greatness], hast thou also brought evil upon the widow with whom I sojourn, by slaying her son?" (1 Kings 17:20). Elijah raises the widow's question: "Did you mean to bring evil upon the widow?" The evil was more than emotional. The son of an elderly widow was her ordinary means of support.

Elijah spread himself on the child and prayed for the restoration of his life. "O Lord my God [the same expression], I pray thee, let this child's soul come into him again" (v. 21). He does so three times before the child revives. (Repetition of a prayer would also be necessary later on Mount Carmel.) Elijah then brings the living child down from his chamber and delivers him to his mother.

Don't you love the prophet's words? "See, thy son liveth" (v. 23). Why the "See"? Was her head buried in her hands, in her arms? Had she turned away not daring to look? Was she sunk in bitterness and wanted nothing more to do with Elijah and his God? Elijah was the prophet of great announcements, and none for her was greater than this. The restoration of the widow's son to his mother is the first instance in Scripture of a person's being brought back from the dead.

We learn something of the human makeup from the way the renewal of life is described. Elijah prayed that "this child's soul would come into him again." The writer then tells us that "the LORD heard the voice of Elijah; and the soul of the child came into him again, and he revived" (v. 22). The body's life is dependent upon the soul but the soul's life is independent of the body. Still the body is referred to as "him." This is a difficult concept. Our bodies are not our essential selves and yet they are part of our complete selves. We can exist without our bodies, but God did not intend that to be our normative state.

The widow's spirits rise, after a double whiplash, in a stirring confession of belief. "Now by this I know that thou art a man of God, and that the word of the LORD in thy mouth is truth" (v. 24). The miraculous reviving of her son had accomplished its work in the confirmation of her tentative faith. The Lord God of Israel had been, up to this time in her mind, "the LORD *thy* God." Now it appears that Elijah's God has become her God too. What God takes away with one hand He can give back with the other.

The function of this episode in the overarching story is now clear. Will a grander display of Jehovah's power on a mountain before His own people achieve a comparable result? The prostrate Elijah stretched on the child calling upon God for his renewal of life and God's miraculous answer followed by the widow's confession of belief picture what could and should happen in the great event to come. The renewal of life shows what God wished to do on a national scale for a repentant Israel.

BACK TO ISRAEL

We don't know when in the three years or so Elijah spent in Sidon the restoration of the widow's son occurred. First Kings 18 opens with God commanding His official representative and messenger to return to the drought-stricken land, present himself to the wicked king, and tell him "I will send rain upon the earth" (v. 1). Notice the form of the announcement: "I will send." Israel's true God is saying that He, not Baal, is the rain god and that He has determined it is time to end the drought. The issue is framed as a quite personal one between competing divinities.

The drought has become especially acute in Samaria. Ahab is taking final measures to save what's become of his kingdom. He is going to scour the kingdom to "find grass to save the horses and mules alive" (v. 5). Notice the minimalism. We think of the widow's gathering a couple of sticks by the city gate to make a fire to bake the last of her flour for her and her son and then die. But Ahab's concern is evidently for mounts for his court and military personnel, not for his suffering people. The character of a person reflects that of the God he serves.

OBADIAH

Now a figure we haven't met appears abruptly on the scene. Ahab enlists his house steward and chief subordinate to help him find springs and brooks that are still running with bordering vegetation they can collect for the royal animals. They will divide the kingdom between them.

The royal servant is Obadiah. His name means "servant of Jehovah." Elijah, whose name means "Jehovah is my God," intercepts him. Notice the play on the lordness theme in his response to Elijah—Obadiah "fell on his face" (v. 7)—and in their exchange of words. "Art thou that my lord Elijah?" "I am: go tell thy lord, Behold, Elijah is here." "What have I sinned, that thou wouldest deliver thy servant into the hand of Ahab, to slay me? As the Lord thy God liveth, there is no nation or kingdom, whither my lord hath not sent to seek thee" (v. 7–10), and so forth.

Obadiah, "servant of Jehovah," is a servant of Ahab, his earthly lord, and addresses Elijah, "Jehovah is my God," as "my lord Elijah" and again as "my lord." He is troubled when Elijah tells him, "Go tell thy lord, Behold, Elijah is here" (v. 11). Has his lord Elijah not heard of his hiding a hundred of the Lord's prophets in a cave and keeping them alive during the slaughter of their brethren by Jezebel? "And now thou sayest, Go, tell thy lord, Behold, Elijah is here" (v. 14). Obadiah fears he will be exposed and lose his life.

Notice the antithetical parallelism. Two court ministers meet on official missions, the one sent by an earthly ruler, the lord of northern Israel, the other sent by a heavenly ruler, the Lord of all Israel and nations beyond. Obadiah serves at the behest of Ahab, Elijah at the behest of Jehovah. Obadiah must negotiate conflicting loyalties, to his lord Ahab and his Lord Jehovah. Elijah's obligation is single, simple—to the Lord of heaven, ruler of all territories and kingdoms including Ahab's. We are admitted to the push and pull within Obadiah's mind. We have no need to be admitted to Elijah's mind; he has no inner conflict like Obadiah's. To be centered and single in one's servanthood is to bestow on oneself the gift of a simple life. Godly commitment is an elegant antidote to moral and psychological confusion.

Elijah responds with the same oath formula with which he began his announcement of the drought to Ahab: "As the LORD of hosts liveth, before whom I stand, I will surely shew myself unto him to day" (v. 15). The ironies shout from this passage. It advances the lordness theme that runs through these separate episodes. Who is Obadiah's lord? Who is Israel's lord? We shall see. What wonderful staging we have here for the climactic confrontation to follow.

Some ambiguities remain. Perhaps we should not be too severe on Obadiah. It is common to think of him as a failed witness, a coward. Prophets, we think, are not supposed to be in hiding during a time of spiritual conflict. But Elijah himself was sent by God into hiding for the time being. Did Israel during these years of drought deserve a bold public proclamation of the truth? That would come in due time. Obadiah had put his life in Elijah's hands to serve his God.

It is also striking that a genuine resourceful worshiper of Jehovah was elevated to so high a position that he could be protecting God's interests and preserving true religion right under the nose of an Ahab. Just as Jehovah had penetrated Sidon in the person of Elijah with the widow and her household, so His presence had penetrated the palace in Samaria in the person of the most trusted servant of the king. If Obadiah were exposed, those he was protecting would be exposed with him.

7

ELIJAH'S SECOND CONFRONTATION

Ahab, having been informed by Obadiah of Elijah's appearance in the kingdom and assured that Elijah would remain in the same spot till he arrived, accosts the prophet with threatening words: "Art thou he that troubleth Israel?" (1 Kings 18:17). The idea that Elijah has brought trouble on the kingdom is so absurd it hardly merits a reply. Ahab has searched the country and surrounding countries to find the prophet. Did he think Elijah had cast a spell on the land? Attributing this power to Elijah contradicted Ahab's support of Baal worship. If Baal were the god of Israel who sent rain, why search the world to find the prophet responsible for stopping the rain?

Elijah counters wonderfully with the real cause, the wicked rejection of Israel's true God and departure from His commandments. What is more irrational than one party to a covenant defaulting on his part and then after things go wrong blaming the other party for not keeping the bargain? What is more pathetically human than that?

Just as in a Greek tragedy, two champions have confronted each other. Unlike a Greek tragedy, one of them, Ahab, quickly gives way to the other.

At this point we can understand the length and detail given to the story of Obadiah. The story gives us his name, tells us about him, has him tell us the same things about himself, records his conversation, and then has him disappear from the scene. Why all this attention to so inconsequential a character? Why doesn't the story simply skip to Elijah's confrontation with Ahab? We believe that Bible narratives contain no wasted motion.

Surely the answer is that Obadiah is a foil to Elijah. He is to Ahab as Elijah is to Israel's Lord God. Obadiah introduces himself to Elijah as Ahab's court minister and emissary with an official duty, to find water for the horses and mules. Elijah introduced himself to Ahab three years before as Jehovah's court minister and emissary with an official duty, a message to deliver.

But the ironic parallels don't end there. From verse 17 on, Elijah is in charge, giving commands to Ahab, and Ahab is, as it were, Elijah's court minister carrying out orders from Elijah and Elijah's God. Ahab responds like an under agent of the court of Jehovah, Elijah's lackey. There will soon be a momentous showdown, and arrangements have to be made. It is Ahab's duty to set the table, as we might say, for great doings in the offing.

SHOWDOWN

Ahab is directed to summon all the prophets of Baal to Baal's great high place on Mount Carmel. Baal's altar is already there, perhaps also groves of trees sacred to Baal's consort Ashtoreth, concealing ritual licentiousness. Mount Carmel is a high ridge looking out over the Mediterranean where "the effects of the drought would be least apparent and the power of Baal to nurture life would seem to be strongest."[1] Ahab obediently sets the stage for Elijah. Then he like Obadiah will disappear from view.

Elijah explains the purpose of the contest. It will identify the true God of Israel. "How long halt ye between two opinions? If the LORD be God, follow him: but if Baal, then follow him." Notice the dramatic touch. "And the people answered him not a word" (v. 21). They are waiting. We are too.

---

1. *Zondervan KJV Study Bible* (Grand Rapids: Zondervan, 1995), 486.

Elijah has stacked the odds humanly in the Baal worshipers' favor: one prophet of Jehovah against four hundred fifty prophets of Baal, not including the prophets of the groves. He sets the rules impartially. Let them take a calf, cut it in pieces, and lay it on the wood without fire. You call on the name of your gods and I'll call on the name of the Lord, "and the God that answereth by fire, let him be God" (v. 24). How reasonable. Who could object?

Now the people do speak, approving Elijah's proposal, "It is well spoken" (v. 24). Elijah has his audience with him, focused on the outcome. We are being led along step by step by a master storyteller in a suspenseful account of one of the very greatest events in biblical history.

If Jehovah answers by fire, it will not be the first time. Recall the descending of fire on the altar at Aaron's dedication of the tabernacle and also on the altar at the dedication of Solomon's temple. But Elijah had no access to the temple in Jerusalem. This drama is being played out at a pagan worship site. Like Elijah's visit to the widow of Sidon in the territory ruled by Jezebel's father, his appearance on Carmel has taken him deep into Baal territory. Carmel is in northwestern Israel, a small distance below Tyre.

Notice the detail with which the narrator renders the increasing agitation of the Baal prophets. Their frenzied, frantic dancing and wild cries gain them only dead silence, the silence of false religion. They leap upon their altar, offering themselves as sacrifices to Baal's fire from heaven. They continue throughout the morning while the people watch. But to no purpose. "There was no voice, nor any that answered" (v. 26). Heartbreaking words these are, that speak to us of the pathetic efforts of millions even today to secure answers from heaven in their designated sacred spots throughout the world.

At noon Elijah breaks his silence and begins to taunt. "Call loudly. He is a god and [therefore] he may be talking [or be occupied], or pursuing [or have stepped aside], or is on a journey, or is sleeping and needs to be waked up" (v. 27, author's paraphrase). This is not the case with the One "that keepeth Israel," who "shall neither slumber nor sleep" (Ps. 121:4). The ecstatic dancing and raving intensifies and the Baal prophets cut themselves with lances and swords till their blood pours out. Surely Baal will notice human blood.

This continues to no avail until the evening. They have been at it all day to no purpose. "There was neither voice, nor any to answer, nor any that regarded" (1 Kings 18:29). Notice the expansion of the earlier comment on their success by noonday. There was not only no answer. There was not anyone to answer. There was no one who regarded. It is hard to imagine a more eloquent expression of the emptiness of pagan religion, including false belief in Christian guise. Baal worship had been given every opportunity to prove itself and had come up empty.

Elijah has set the options. The options, if accepted, are consequential, personally for the people and nationally for Israel: "How long halt ye between two opinions?" (v. 21). Jesus said much the same when He uttered the challenge, "No man can serve two masters: for either he will hate the one, and love the other; or else he will hold to the one, and despise the other" (Matt. 6:24). Elijah's word "halt" is the same word in Hebrew for "leaped" in 1 Kings 18:26, which is also defined as "to hesitate" or "to limp" as "limp between two opinions."[2]

I call it the Baal wobble. Northern Israel needs to make up its mind. It's the lordness question we've been following in these chapters. Are there Christians limping along with the Baal wobble? Or dancing between options, swinging wildly back and forth? This is the challenge of this episode. It is old Joshua's farewell challenge to Israel. "Choose you this day whom ye will serve." He had chosen. "As for me and my house, we will serve the LORD" (Josh. 24:15).

"Who is the Lord?" is a question to put to ourselves. It has two parts. "Who in reality is the Lord?" and "Will He be my

---

2. *Strong's Concordance*, s.v. "leaped" H6452, accessed November 25, 2019, https://www.blueletterbible.org/lang/Lexicon/Lexicon.cfm?strongs=H6452&t=KJV.

Lord?" The first part addresses the head. The second part addresses the heart. The Baal wobble is the conflict of the Christian between his two natures, the spirit and the flesh. "The flesh lusteth [desireth, urgeth] against the Spirit, and the Spirit against the flesh: and these are contrary the one to the other: so that ye cannot do the things that ye would" (Gal. 5:17).

After the Baal prophets have done all they can, probably to the point of exhaustion (the wild dancing must have taken all four hundred and fifty of them to keep it going), Elijah calls the business to a halt and takes over. There will be no loud summoning of his God.

The episode presents a study in contrasts. Notice the calm deliberation with which Elijah goes about his task—the care with which he prepares the site and his exact ordering of the sacrifice. The details will recall the people's common identity with the tribes of the southern kingdom. This will be an Israelite sacrifice, absent the altar and temple surroundings, as far as can be performed at a pagan site of worship. Jehovah has invaded Baal.

God's true prophet "took twelve stones, according to the number of the tribes of the sons of Jacob, unto whom the word of the LORD came, saying, Israel shall be thy name: and with the stones he built an altar in the name of the LORD" (1 Kings 18:31–32). The twelve stones for the twelve tribes of Israel are a reminder to his audience of their true identity, politically, socially, and religiously. They belong to larger Israel ruled from Jerusalem. Like the tribe of Judah from which they split off, they were named after the patriarch Jacob. "Israel [Jacob] shall be thy name" (v. 31). The details of this preparation are a rebuke to the people gathered, a stern reminder of who they really are and should consider themselves to be, and under whose rule, spiritually as well as politically, they belong.

Elijah is going to make the offering harder to burn. There will be no tricks. He will douse it with water to elevate the challenge and increase the proof. Water is precious, especially on a mountaintop. It would have to be transported up. He digs a trench around the altar to keep the water collected. It will contain about six gallons. He calls for four gallons of water to be poured on the wood and on the sacrifice three times and fills the trench with water. The sacrifice, altar, wood, and surrounding earth are drenched. Elijah has not only been building an altar; he has been piling up evidence—what will become overwhelming evidence.

We are given a description of the sacrifice as specified in Leviticus 1:7. "He put the wood in order" (1 Kings 18:33). The wood was to be precisely arranged. Careful readers of Scripture are impressed by God's attention to arrangement and system. He is a God of order. We should care about structure and discipline in the things of God. Beauty is part of it; I suspect there was deliberate patterning and even symmetry in the way the wood was placed.

This care for how the wood was arranged speaks to me symbolically of a life given to God. Christians may become tangled in disorder, but they don't want to be, and they will take any opportunity to escape it. Creation moved from chaos to cosmos. God's forming of a life does the same. Discipline in the home structures the life of a child so he can order his own life someday in the ways of God.

Now the moment has come. It was deliberately chosen. It is "the time of the offering of the evening sacrifice" (v. 36), the time specified in the Mosaic law. The evening sacrifice was just then being performed by the priests in Jerusalem. Elijah had timed it so as to coordinate with the temple worship and with the God of the temple worship that northern Israel had spurned. It would return Israel to her God and even reunite the two kingdoms, he thought. It would return the rain.

DEMONSTRATION AND JUDGMENT

Elijah cries out to the "Lord God of Abraham, Isaac, and of Israel" (v. 36) using the more formal name of Israel retained by the northern kingdom after its split from Judah but in fact historically designating the entire nation. He calls for a vindication of his claim for Jehovah as Israel's true God and for himself as God's messenger. He prays that the people will understand the point of what is going to happen: "that thou hast turned their heart back again" (v. 37).

Then the demonstration happens with an absoluteness that demolishes any possible claims of the authority of Baal and delegitimizes Baal worship once and for all. Or so Elijah had every reason to think. "The fire of the LORD fell" (v. 38), consuming not only the sacrifice and the wood but also the stones, the surrounding earth, and the water in the trench. Elijah's thoroughness in preparing the site with difficulties for the fire served the witness of the demonstration. The people went down on their faces in a posture of worship, but doubtless also from fright, and cried "The LORD, he is the God; the LORD, he is the God" (v. 39). Jehovah abandoned by Israel is Israel's true God and the God as well of the Baal country beyond.

Elijah wasn't finished. Israel was a theocracy, and he had renewed Israel's covenant with God. (The earlier covenant was enacted on a mountain also.) Under Mosaic law, perpetrators of idolatry were to be destroyed. Baal worship was hideously wicked and cruel. Elijah had the people bring the prophets down to the brook Kishon at the foot of Carmel and slay them there. This is the second brook in the story. It may have been mostly dry then. If so, it would not stay dry. A torrent would soon wash the bodies into the sea.

Our thoughts may take us back hundreds of years earlier to a famous Israelite victory over a Canaanite coalition in the same location, celebrated in memorable lines by Deborah and Barak. "They fought from heaven; the stars in their courses fought against Sisera. The river of Kishon swept them away, that ancient river, the river Kishon" (Judg. 5:20–21). Storm and flood had turned the chosen battlefield, the plain of Jezreel drained by Kishon and its tributaries, into swampy terrain, neutralizing the Canaanite chariots stuck in the muddy flats. The river had served Israel before. Pagan storm gods had failed Israel's enemy before. Whereas in Judges the godly prophetess Deborah inspires and enacts Israel's military victory, in the history recorded in 1 Kings the wicked Sidonian princess Jezebel has enacted Israel's spiritual defeat.

Here is an example for us in this series of events. In the revival of persons as well as nations, if spiritual change is truly genuine, repentance will be followed by direct action. After acknowledgment and confession is fierce indignation against the sin responsible for the need for revival. There is zealous and jealous anger against what has offended God and held back His blessing.

Accordingly Paul commends the Corinthians for taking action against the sin in their midst he had identified in a former epistle. They "sorrowed after a godly sort." He was gratified to hear of their response. "What carefulness it wrought in you, yea, what clearing of yourselves, yea, what indignation, yea, what fear, yea what vehement desire, yea, what zeal, yea what revenge!" (2 Cor. 7:11). The Corinthian Christians had gone to war against the disobedience that cost them God's blessing. Now would come refreshing.

THE RAIN AND RETURN

After the slaughter of the Baal prophets, Elijah tells Ahab, "Get thee up, eat and drink; for there is a sound of abundance of rain" (1 Kings 18:41). There were no clouds as yet. Was there distant thunder audible only to Elijah? Was it heard only privately in his spirit, attuned by God? In any case, Ahab does as he is told, leaving the carnage at the foot of Carmel "to eat and drink." (Has he been fasting with the prophets of Baal?) Elijah ascends the mountain to pray. So Moses came down from Sinai with God's covenant only to find idolatry, slay the perpetrators, and then reascend to the top.

On the top of Carmel Elijah takes a posture of earnest prayer. "He cast himself down upon the earth, and put his face between his knees" (v. 42). This is the posture of formal prayer today in Middle Eastern temples and mosques, but here to the extreme— "his face between his knees"! His bodily posture had imaged the posture of his soul when he was stretched over the lifeless widow's son begging God for his breath to return. Outer posture can reflect inner posture. It can even affect it. We read our own bodies and assimilate to what they picture to us of ourselves.

Elijah prays and sends his servant to look for signs of rain. We don't have the words of his prayer as we have with his prayer for the widow's son. But the immediate effect, or lack of effect, is identical. The servant looks toward the sea and returns with the report, "There is nothing." Notice that the words "There is" in verse 43 are in italics. The servant was brief. "Nothing!" Elijah praying in a posture of extreme urgency, stretched over the widow's son, saw no result until the third time. How often do we succumb to discouragement after our first effort in prayer when we look for the answer and "there is nothing." We have a prayer lesson here. Would God get the fellowship He wants from us if He always immediately answered our prayers?

That of course was not the cause of God's delays on behalf of Elijah. He may have been staging His response by a momentary suspense. This episode would have multitudes of readers and hearers in millennia to come. But then we don't know why Elijah had to repeat his prayer three times for the return of a boy's life and seven times for the return of the rain. "Go again" was Elijah's response each time to the servant, and it can well be God's response to our discouragement as well.

The seventh time the servant returned he had something but not very much to build a hope upon. "Behold, there ariseth a little cloud out of the sea, like a man's hand" (v. 44). The servant could report only smallness, a little hand-shaped cloud, like the widow's "handful of meal and little oil," available to relieve a desperate need. But that was the evidence Elijah was waiting for, and he sprang into action. He sends his servant to Ahab, with welcome orders: "Prepare thy chariot, and get thee down, that the rain stop thee not" (v. 44). The momentum of the story accelerates. Like the rain, its forward motion has been restrained. New energies are being released. Notice the power of the description. "And it came to pass in the mean while, that the heaven was black with clouds and wind, and there was a great rain" (v. 45).

Ahab rode in his chariot to Jezreel, his summer palace. God had a final wonder for the king and his people. "The hand of the Lord was on Elijah; and he girded up his loins, and ran before Ahab to the entrance of Jezreel" (v. 46), a marathon distance. To stay ahead of the king's chariot, Elijah must have been running at well more than marathon speed. I see here a divine generosity in God's honoring of Elijah the man and a final validation of the prophet's great work. God gives Elijah a little additional glory in the miraculous enabling of his run.

The upstaged Ahab could not expect the same. Awaiting Elijah's royal facilitator—the no doubt reluctant instrument of his orders and the cowed implementer of his plan—was not glory but the ferocity of the queen.

DISAPPOINTMENT AND DEJECTION

Up to this point we have not been given an inside view of Elijah such as God gives us of the prophet Jeremiah and to an extent of Jonah. This powerful figure larger than life breaks into the Old Testament narrative with an enormous impact, dominating Ahab and his court, and disappears. Afterward we see God taking care of Elijah, and then the widow and her son and Elijah being greatly affected by the boy's death. He is God's choice to recall to northern Israel the covenant dating from Sinai and to renew that covenant on a mountain within the land, calling the people to repentance. He comes in a formal role as a court emissary with a declaration. We may think of that other "man sent from God, whose name was John" (John 1:6). Both expected their messages to unite the nation and turn it back to God. Both were bitterly disappointed and needed encouragement from God, Elijah from an angel, John the Baptist from the Lord. Elijah, James tells us, "was a man subject to like passions as we are" (James 5:17). As we shall see, he could be as fearful at some times as he was bold at others.

After Elijah's return from Carmel, the pace of events picks up. Immediately a message came to Elijah from Jezebel. It was a threat on his life backed by an oath. It was retaliation for Elijah's slaughter of the Baal prophets. "So let the gods do to me, and more also, if I make not thy life as the life of one of them by tomorrow about this time" (1 Kings 19:2). Ironically, it would not be Elijah who would die that day. Jezebel, by her oath, was pronouncing her own death, and her death would be worse than that of the Baal prophets.

Elijah fled to the south, as far as he could go and still be in the land of Israel. Beersheba was the jumping off point for an Israelite travelling to Egypt. It was rich in patriarchal associations. But Elijah didn't stay there. He kept going a day's journey into the wilderness and lay and slept under a desert shrub.

How much of his flight was due to the fear of Jezebel (she and Ahab had no jurisdiction over southern Israel, here named Judah) is not easy to determine. We read that he was fleeing for his life, and that was of course the case. But Elijah seems demoralized and deeply depressed from the failure of his mission (v. 10). The words in verse 4 prayed in exhaustion under the desert shrub indicate he wants to die. "It is enough. . . . I am not better than my fathers."

Surely he is referring to what seemed the final defeat of Baal on Mount Carmel which had turned out to be not final after all. All his energies, his claims for his God, his expectations, his faith, must have seemed now pointless. Elijah had rebuilt an altar to the Lord God of Israel on Mount Carmel. Now the Lord God of Israel must rebuild Elijah. How He will go about it is interesting.

THE GENTLENESS OF GOD

Elijah is wakened from his sleep under the juniper bush by an angel, who tells him to "arise and eat" (v. 5). What did he see? "He looked, and, behold, there was a cake baken on the coals, and a cruse of water at his head" (v. 6). (Where have we seen such a thing before? Recall the little cake the widow of Zarepthah was going to bake for her and her son before they died.) They were "at his head," impossible to miss.

He eats and goes back to sleep. After a while the angel wakes him again and tells him to eat more. He has a long journey.

Recall Elijah's instruction to Ahab at the foot of Carmel, "Get thee up, eat and drink; for there is a sound of abundance of rain" (18:41).

Notice the link between physical deprivation and a troubled mind. There is a school of thought in Christian psychology that physical factors are not the real problem in depression, and that emotional disturbances are entirely under spiritual governance. No Christian would dispute the importance of the spiritual. But God does not rule out natural causation in emotional disturbances or natural means in the restoring of a mind. Here natural means, nourishment and rest, are backed by the word of an angel. Elijah rests, eats and drinks, rests some more, eats and drinks some more, and gets something to do. That's good psychology, good therapy. Elijah is a weakened man.

Elijah takes a forty-day journey farther south into the Sinai desert until he comes to "Horeb the mount of God" (v. 8). This is another name for Mount Sinai from which Israel under Moses had received the Law and covenanted with God to keep it. The mountain had rumbled and quaked and burned dreadfully while Moses was representing Israel before God and God before Israel. Now Elijah, who had represented God to his people on a mountain and conducted a sort of little Sinai on the summit, renewing their covenant with a demonstration of fire, is going to get his own demonstration. It will be different.

Elijah comes to the sacred mount and finds a cave to settle in. The Sinai mountains are riddled with caves. They offer protection from the heat. God is going to attend to his discouragement. The language of verses 9 and 13 raises a question whether Elijah should have been there at all. Perhaps the key is the word *lodge*. God meant him to take shelter in a cave. Where else could he go? But Elijah may have slipped into a more permanent state of mind. He had prayed earlier, "It is enough: . . . take away my life" (v. 4). That was an error, though an understandable one. God is jealous of His authority to determine when "it is enough." He knows what He has in mind for the duration of a life.

Whereas the word of the Lord has come to Elijah concerning His enemies, now it comes to Elijah concerning himself. It comes in the form of a question: "What doest thou here, Elijah?" (v. 9). There is tenderness here. God wants Elijah to formulate an explanation and to consider his explanation. Let's not be too quick to condemn Elijah. Elijah is beaten down. God is kinder than some preachers. There is tenderness here in this rebuke, if it is a rebuke, and I'm not entirely sure it is.

We don't use questions enough with our children or in addressing problems with friends. I remember my father saying so many times, "Ronnie, was that kind?" I know a young woman who was leaning away from returning to her Christian university. I knew she was troubled about the direction of her life but resistant to my direction. I asked her about the state of her thinking. "Are you sure you know your mind about next fall?" She said, "No," and I was able to lead her from there. The question God put to Elijah could have had a variety of tones. What do you suppose was the tone in which God's question was delivered here?

Elijah spills out his frustration and disillusionment. He has been consumed by the mind of God toward Israel. Notice his total identification with God's view. "I have been very jealous for the LORD God of hosts: for the children of Israel [Jacob's descendants] have forsaken thy covenant, thrown down thine altars, and slain thy prophets with the sword; and I, even I only, am left; and they seek my life, to take it away" (v. 10). Notice the violence of God's enemies here. Elijah fears that his death will complete their victory over Israel's true God. That, I think, is his greatest discouragement and greatest fear.

God tells Elijah to "go forth, and stand upon the mount" before Him (v. 11). God means to give Elijah a Sinai-type demonstration prepared precisely for him. It will include rock-tearing wind, an earthquake, and fire—phenomena Elijah associated with the character of God and His actions. God will not be in these however. God can act in quiet, no less persuasive, ways, as indeed He was doing here with his prophet servant.

"A still small voice" (v. 12) calls Elijah to the mouth of the cave. He covers his face with his mantle, since he is to have a conversation with God. Again he hears again the former question, "What doest thou here, Elijah?" (v. 13). The prophet replies with the same words as before. Then the conversation ends. God does not reply to Elijah's response but gives him something to do. There is wisdom for counselors here.

God counters Elijah's depression, a third one, with another commission. He is to "return on [his] way" (v. 15) (a depressed person needs to hear those words) and do three things. He is to anoint a new king of Syria, anoint the next king of Israel, and anoint his prophet successor. Both prophets will continue God's judgment of Israel. Elijah's witness to the true God will not cease under Elisha.

Elijah is also given some information to cheer him. "Yet I have left me seven thousand in Israel, all the knees which have not bowed unto Baal, and every mouth which hath not kissed him" (v. 18). In the Hebrew idiom, seven thousand can mean in round terms very, very many.

Elijah fulfilled only one of these three tasks. He never anointed Hazael or Jehu. Elisha would tell Hazael he would be king and would send a prophet to anoint Jehu. God had kindly allowed the dejected Elijah to withdraw. He had also encouraged Elijah with the assurance that his witness to Israel and God's judgment of Israel would not end with him.

We learn much of Elijah in these incidents but also much of our gracious God. Jehovah outdoes Baal as a storm god, but shows Himself Baal's utter opposite in His care for His own. He leaves Elijah in a cave to introspect for a while, then calls him to the mouth of the cave and shows him Himself. There is theological weight in this story; it trumpets the goodness and greatness of God.

ELISHA

The narrative settles briefly on the third task given to Elijah at Sinai by the Lord, the one he actually performed. The three tasks were anointings of successors, the first two of future kings and the third of a future prophet. Notice the odd way in which Elisha's ministry is grouped with the others. "And it shall come to pass, that him that escapeth from the sword of Hazael shall Jehu slay: and him that escapeth from the sword of Jehu shall Elisha slay" (19:17). The Lord chooses to emphasize this feature of Elisha's prophetic work. It will continue the role of Elijah as a messenger and enactor of judgment on evil in Israel. This revelation to Elijah is encouragement to him that his work has not ended in defeat. It has not reached a sad conclusion.

Verse 19 shows Elijah seeking out Elisha and in a symbolic gesture identifying him as his successor.

The details are interesting. Elijah walks by while Elisha is plowing, tosses his mantle on him, and keeps going. There is nothing formal about it. There is no persuasion offered to Elisha, no opportunity held out before him, no obligation laid on him to respond. What we have is a simple act of commissioning with an anticipated but not required response.

How very much like the call of the disciples recounted in John 1 is this of Elisha. John the Baptist is speaking with two of his disciples; Jesus walks by, entering their field of vision; they leave what they are doing and follow Him. "And he left the oxen, and ran after Elijah" (v. 20). Elijah was evidently a distance down the road. Elisha had to catch up with him. Elisha left what he was doing, the mantle flapping behind him (my thought), to follow his master. He would be Elijah's servant. That mantle, like Moses's rod, would serve him well in the work to which he was called. As in the anointings of Jehu and Hazael, it bespoke royalty.

Elijah was not in an accommodating mode. He anointed his successor. His successor had to pick up the initiative, to demonstrate resolve. And so he did. There was however an interval. Elisha asked for a delay. "Let me, I pray thee, kiss my father and my mother, and then I will follow thee." Elijah's reply was not encouraging: "Go back again: for what have I done to thee?"

(v. 20). Matthew 8:21–22 puts Elisha's request for more time in a bad light. Or does it?

I find nothing that is not admirable in Elisha's request for a delay in his call. Notice the description. He "was plowing with twelve yoke of oxen before him, and he with the twelfth" (v. 19), possibly overseeing servants who were plowing with the other eleven teams. He was working the family land. He could not just drop his work and leave the animals in the field. He had undertaken responsibility. He also desired to honor his parents with a heartfelt, abundant farewell.

Compare him with the would-be disciple in Matthew 8 who wanted to remain at home until his parents died. I think this request is a tribute to the kind of family Elisha had. Notice that his father is identified twice when Elisha is introduced in the story—an honoring in Holy Writ.

AN AFTERLIFE

The stories of the Bible are full of surprises. It would seem that God had brought Elijah's prophetic life to a gentle close. He had given Elijah a threefold commission, two parts of which he did not fulfill. The third part was an anointing of a successor, symbolized by the relinquishing of his mantle. Elijah under the juniper bush by Beersheba and in the cave at Sinai had lost his will to continue. His mission, he thought, had failed. There were no other prophets left to raise voices for God. The providing of a successor seemed to both counter and confirm his discouragement. There would be another prophet like himself, but that prophet could expect no company and no lasting victory—or so we can imagine his state of mind.

But Elijah's story was not ready to end. We read of Elisha, after his return from his family gathering, "Then he arose, and went after Elijah, and ministered to him" (v. 21). God through an angel and then in person had ministered to Elijah at Beersheba and Sinai. Now God was giving Elijah not only a successor but a ministering servant and protégé. Elisha would be helping his new master while learning from him. The old prophet still had business to do. His old adversary and his queen were still in power in Israel. Elijah was not ready for retirement just yet.

Chapter 20 of 1 Kings does not refer to Elijah except obliquely in countering his pessimistic account of spiritual prospects in Israel. He had spoken of himself as the only prophet to have escaped the terror of Jezebel, and yet "a certain man of the sons of the prophets" (v. 35) confronts Ahab about sparing the defeated king of Syria "whom I appointed to utter destruction" (v. 42). In a later battle Ahab's own life would not be spared. The point for us here is that God had prepared another prophet to challenge Ahab's wickedness. Elijah was not the only prophet available for the truth of God. Jezebel had not slain them all.

8

ELIJAH'S THIRD CONFRONTATION

First Kings 21 records another great moment for Elijah. Once again he appears boldly on a public stage in confrontation with his old adversary Ahab. His spirit has not left him. It has revived in full flame. Ahab and Jezebel are in Jezreel where they have a palace closer than Samaria to Jezebel's home. It is also a fortified city at the edge of the great plain where major battles have been fought with Israel's enemies to the north. It has military importance.

Ahab wants a privately owned vineyard next to his palace for a vegetable garden. He is willing to exchange it with the owner for another better garden. The owner, Naboth, refuses to sell it since it belongs to him by family inheritance. It is his patrimony, probably descending to him from the tribal distribution of lands in Israel under Joshua. These lands were meant to stay with their owners. It was contrary to Mosaic law to transfer their ownership, particularly to a family of another tribe. Naboth was not only entitled traditionally to his land; there may have been legal constraint on him as well.

Ahab returns to his palace in a sulk. The phrase "heavy and displeased" describes him after his rebuke by the prophet in 1 Kings 20:43 (again in 21:4). He wasn't used to being blocked. (Note: what causes one to be "heavy and displeased" can say a great deal about one's character as well as about one's ability to handle disappointment.) Jezebel seems amazed that her husband would let himself be frustrated by the will of a subject: "Dost thou now govern the kingdom of Israel?" (v. 7). Again the lordness theme—who rules in Israel?

Jezebel writes letters proclaiming a fast, pays two men of the lowest sort to accuse Naboth of blaspheming Israel's God (not Baal!), and has him condemned and stoned. She tells Ahab he can rise from his bed and take possession of the vineyard. We read "that Ahab rose up to go down to the vineyard" (v. 16). Indeed he did get up to go down.

Word next comes to Elijah the Tishbite (notice the same form of reference that introduced him before): "Arise, go down to meet Ahab king of Israel" who "is in the vineyard of Naboth, whither he is gone down to possess it" (v. 18). And God gives Elijah a chilling message, with coarse words, to drive home the evil of Ahab and Jezebel's act and the dire judgment that awaits them.

Burial with dignity and a noble legacy was the fitting end of a splendid rule. Nothing less would be thinkable for Israel's king and for his Phoenician queen. But Ahab has sold "himself to work wickedness in the sight of the LORD," a ruler disposed to work evil, "whom Jezebel his wife stirred up" (v. 25). He will return to the vineyard of Naboth in Jezreel but not pleasantly. "In the place where dogs licked the blood of Naboth shall dogs lick thy blood, even thine" (v. 19). (See verse 29 for the response of the Lord to Ahab's repentence.) Of Jezebel said the Lord, "The dogs shall eat Jezebel by the wall of Jezreel" (v. 23).

So also it would be of Ahab's fleeing army. "Him that dieth of Ahab in the city the dogs shall eat; and him that dieth in the field shall the fowls of the air eat" (v. 24). The remains of Ahab's vaunted rule would be dog dung and vulture droppings. The dam of God's wrath on the royal line of Ahab would burst, and its rottenness would defile the ground. Let's never forget both "the goodness and severity of God" (Rom. 11:22).

But the point for us in our reading is the revival of Elijah's prophetic power. God graciously gave him a magnificent sequel to the triumph on Carmel. God was not about to let this great servant slink miserably away, the victim of his dejection. God will reaffirm a life when a person cannot find in himself the ability to do so.

AHAB'S REPENTANCE

Two of the greatest surprises in Old Testament history are the spiritual U-turns of the two wickedest kings in Israel's and Judah's histories, Ahab and Manasseh. "There was none like unto Ahab, which did sell himself to work wickedness in the sight of the LORD, whom Jezebel his wife stirred up" (1 Kings 21:25). But after Elijah's prophecy against Ahab, the king "rent his clothes, and put sackcloth upon his flesh, and fasted, and lay in sackcloth, and went softly" (v. 27). (Compare his earlier lying on his bed, face turned away, and refusal to eat after Naboth's refusal to sell him his vineyard.)

Amazingly God credited his repentance and revised the prophesied judgment. The evil on his house would come not in his days but in his son's days. His royal line would end not with him but with the second of his sons to take the throne. Also the dogs would lick the blood of his chariot in the pool of Samaria rather than in Naboth's former vineyard. That detail would be fulfilled in the slaying of his younger son, Jehoram, successor to his elder son, Ahaziah, making a final end to Ahab's royal house, the house of Omri. (See 2 Kings 9 for the story and its parallels with the death of Ahab.) Just as Elijah's ministry seemed to him to be over and wasn't, so the life and royal line of Ahab seemed to be over as prophesied and wasn't. Ahab would live another three years. Ahaziah survived Ahab two years; Jehoram survived Ahaziah twelve years. Then the other seventy sons of Ahab would be slaughtered by Jehu.

9

ELIJAH'S FOURTH CONFRONTATION

Elijah has outlived Ahab and will outlive Ahab's elder son, Ahaziah, who followed his father in wickedness and a punitive death. In the first chapter of 2 Kings, Ahaziah has fallen through a lattice ceiling in an upper chamber of his palace and has sent messengers to the Baal shrine at Ekron, the northernmost of the five major cities of Philistia, to learn whether he will recover from his injuries. He has ruled only two years. An angel of God tells Elijah to intercept the messengers and respond to Ahaziah's question. Elijah confronts them, delivers his message verbatim, and leaves.

> Is it not because there is not a God in Israel, that ye go to inquire of Baal-zebub the god of Ekron? Now therefore thus saith the LORD, Thou shalt not come down from that bed on which thou art gone up, but shalt surely die. (2 Kings 1:3–4)

This is indeed astounding. Has this pathetic vile worship been reinstated in Israel so soon after its devastating defeat at Carmel? Baalzebub is here the god of a city. One must travel to hear a word from him. The God of Israel rules more than a city. He has no territorial limits. A person must go to Baalzebub. Israel's God comes to the person, as He does here.

When the messengers turn back to the king with Elijah's message rather than Baalzebub's, the king asks for a description of the prophet: "What manner of man was he which came up to meet you, and told you these words?" (v. 7). They reply, "he was an hairy man, and girt with a girdle of leather about his loins" (v. 8). He was wearing an animal skin, belted with a leather tie. Ahaziah knows of him. "It is Elijah the Tishbite" (v. 8), that old identifying phrase by which he was known to Ahaziah's father and contemporaries.

Ahaziah sends fifty soldiers to take him. They find him sitting "on the top of an hill" (v. 9). I'm impressed with the oddness as well as the goodness of this great man. They address him as a prophet, "Thou man of God," and call him down. Elijah calls fire down. When fifty more are sent, fire consumes them also.

Ahaziah persists and sends still a third group. But this captain ascends to Elijah, falls on his knees, and beseeches him, "O man of God, I pray thee, let my life, and the life of these fifty thy servants, be precious in thy sight. Behold, there came fire down from heaven, and burnt up the two captains of the former fifties with their fifties: therefore let my life now be precious in thy sight" (vv. 13–14). The angel of the Lord tells Elijah, "Go down with him: be not afraid of him. And he arose, and went down with him unto the king" (v. 15) and delivered to Ahaziah verbatim the original message.

It would happen as prophesied by Elijah. "So he died according to the word of the Lord which Elijah had spoken" (v. 17). This simple, matter-of-fact, no-nonsense description is in keeping with the terse, direct manner in which Elijah spoke his messages. The prophet was a simple man of few words. A few were all he ever needed. His message and mission were concentrated on a single idea, which took the form of a question: Who is the God of Israel? He excelled in simple faithfulness.

When his mission seemed in collapse, Elijah was hollowed out, his spirit exhausted. It is one thing to conquer territory. It is quite another to hold the territory that has been conquered. But had his efforts ended in defeat? Have we not seen how very partial was Elijah's view of his life's total arc? God knew much more. He still had work for His beloved servant.

In this fourth and final confrontation with a king and second pronouncement of a death, we can see a continuity in the prophetic career of Elijah. After his flight to the south from Jezebel, he was reassured and revitalized by his God and given important tasks to perform on a royal stage. But there would be a diminishing as he approached his end. The parallels with Carmel are interesting in this fourth of his confrontations with a king. Elijah met Ahaziah's messengers before meeting their king just as he had encountered Obadiah before meeting Ahab. Ahaziah's messengers were lesser in rank than was Obadiah, a prominent court official. Elijah, standing, called down fire on a mountain whereas here he calls down fire while sitting on a hill. Death comes to four hundred fifty priests of Baal at the foot of Mount Carmel; two groups of fifty and their captains perish at the foot of Elisha's hill. Elijah's court appearance before Ahaziah following the fiery demonstration is less dramatic than his sudden appearance to Ahab on the road before the incident at Carmel.

These parallels with contrasts are, I think, meant to tell us something about God's crafting of a life. Beauty and strength naturally subside along with matching opportunities, but not the glory, and God's wonders may not be at an end. There is grandeur in the profile of an old prophet sitting on a hill defying his takers, obeying them only when encouraged to do so by an angel of the Lord. "Be not afraid of him" (v. 15). I think we see something here reminiscent of Elijah's fear of Jezebel. He may in fact have been a naturally fearful man whose fear was mastered by intense conviction and passion for his God. He was "a man subject to like passions as we are," wrote James (5:17). At the end of his recorded exploits, Elijah is still pronouncing on kings and kingdoms but from a lesser stage. Don't we all pray that God will thus graciously and artfully conduct our own descents?

THE GRAND EXIT

A first reader of the Elijah story could not imagine an event in Elijah's life at all comparable to his triumph on Mount Carmel. But such an event comes on suddenly at the beginning of 2 Kings 2 without a buildup. "And it came to pass, when the Lord would take up Elijah into heaven by a whirlwind, that Elijah went with Elisha from Gilgal" (v. 1). Was ever a fact so amazing delivered in so prosaic a way? What follows is not a bare recital of facts however.

Coupled with the astonishing revelation about Elijah is a fact about Elisha that dominates the account. Elisha is with Elijah and is determined to stay by him. The conversation between them may remind us of what passed between Naomi and Ruth when Naomi seemed to be discouraging Ruth from continuing with her to Bethlehem. Elijah tells Elisha to stay behind while he goes to another location. Elisha vows not to leave him. The "sons of the prophets," first at Bethel and then at Jericho, tell him "The LORD will take away thy master from thy head to day," and Elisha tells them "Yea, I know it; hold ye your peace" (v. 3). Here is a kind of ritual buildup for something monumental about to happen. What is emphasized is the resoluteness of Elisha, who evidently is being tested. Constancy, continuance, is the great test of every professing Christian.

Why does Elijah take this particular roundabout route to the river? We can only speculate. Was his journey a farewell to the sons of the prophets? The locations were famous in Israel's history. At Gilgal the tribes under Joshua assembled and were circumcised after crossing the Jordan. It was a staging area for their invasion of Canaan. Its name signified the "roll[ing]" of "the reproach of Egypt from off [them]" in a physical sign (Josh. 5:9). Bethel ("house of God") was the place of Jacob's first vital encounter with God. Ironically it was now the center of the calf worship of northern Israel. Jericho was the location of Israel's most spectacular victory over the Canaanites, which began their invasion of the land. Perhaps because of their religious associations, they had become sites for the nurturing of prophets in a hostile land.

But Gilgal, Bethel, and Jericho were great starting points in Israel's history: Gilgal, a spiritual and physical preparation for conquest; Bethel, a spiritual encounter of the nation's progenitor with God; and Jericho, the first victory in Israel's conquest of the land. There is here a gathering up of consequential events in Israel's national memory that characterize historically the mission of Elijah that Elisha will carry on. The two men complete their circuit and are back at the river Jordan, perhaps not far from where Elijah's prophetic career began. With short, quick strokes the scene is set for us.

"And they two went on. And fifty men of the sons of the prophets went, and stood to view afar off: and they two stood by Jordan" (2 Kings 2:6–7).

Elijah uses his mantle to divide the Jordan as Moses had used his rod to the divide the Red Sea. "They two went over on dry ground" (v. 8) as Joshua and his followers had done on entering Canaan. The narrator evidently is depicting a second Moses and Joshua combined. (Elisha must have returned Elijah's mantle to him, after having it cast upon him, before returning home.)

Elijah says to his companion, "Ask what I shall do for thee, before I be taken away from thee." I recall another time in a period of transition of political power in Israel when a successor is invited by God to ask what He would wish to be given. Here is a transition of spiritual power, and Elisha responds, "I pray thee, let a double portion of thy spirit be upon me" (v. 9).

Some commentators have pointed out that there are almost exactly twice as many recorded miracles by Elisha as by Elijah. Probably the primary reference is to the practice of giving the eldest son a double portion of the inheritance with the responsibility of caring for the remaining parent or parents (if both were still living) and the family lands, while continuing the family name. Elisha knew he needed to possess his master's spiritual power if he were to inherit his master's prophetic mission and responsibility. The one needed to equal the other.

Elijah said, "Thou hast asked a hard thing"—a fascinating reply. Did he mean the power was only God's to give? Or did he mean that the granting of it would bring its recipient great challenges? Elijah states a condition. "If thou see me when I am taken from thee, it shall be so unto thee; but if not, it shall not be so" (v. 10). I'm struck by the conditions raised by Elijah, by the contingency emphasized. Elijah is not making it easy. The granting of the "hard thing" depends on Elisha's response—his persistent exertion.

We have a practice in evangelicalism today that has been with us for many years which has been given a name—*easy-believism*. Salvation certainly is not personally complicated. "By grace are ye saved through faith; and that not of yourselves: it is the gift of God: not of works, lest any man should boast" (Eph. 2:8–9). Some reject salvation for this very reason: because it is too easy. They want to deserve it. It affronts their pride. Others more realistically reject salvation because it is too hard. Salvation assumes commitment, serious discipleship, putting God on the throne of the soul. For these persons, it reaches too far into personal identity and direction of life.

The granting of Elisha's "hard thing" requires his presence with his master. Elisha must shadow Elijah to the end in order to receive Elijah's power, a supernatural endowment Elisha will need in order to carry on his master's ministry after he has gone. Jesus' disciples did not receive the power of their Master until they had shadowed Him three years and seen Him ascend. They then congregated and waited for the power to carry on His work. The first response of true belief is simple and instantaneous, but the "hard thing" has not changed.

I'm interested in the way the momentous here breaks into the mundane. "And it came to pass, as they still went on, and talked, that, behold, there appeared a chariot of fire, and horses of fire, and parted them both asunder; and Elijah went up by a whirlwind into heaven" (2 Kings 2:11). While Elijah and Elisha "still went on and talked," one world—the heavenly—strikes into another, the human world we know. We may think of Jacob's dream at Bethel, when heaven bridged with earth by a stairway. But this was no dream. Its reality could never be doubted. There is that matter of the fallen mantle.

I'm interested in the familiar friendship between the two prophets. Something unimaginable was to happen "as they still went on and talked." Isn't this like God? The mundane routine of your spiritual life can lead to God revealing Himself to you in ways you could never have imagined. I think of old Enoch of whom Scripture records that he "walked with God: and . . . was not; for God took him" (Gen. 5:24).

Chariots get special attention in Israel's history from as far back as Moses's reiteration of the law in Deuteronomy 17:16. Israel's king, when kings were chosen, was not to "multiply horses to himself" (v. 17). (According to verse 17, he was also not to "multiply wives to himself, that his heart turn not away" or "greatly multiply to himself silver and gold.") Horses and chariots with metal axles were then the advanced technology of war, and the glory of Israel was to appear in her reliance on God rather than on the war equipment prized by the enemy nations. Moses's song upon Israel's crossing of the Red Sea on dry land begins, "I will sing unto the LORD, for he hath triumphed gloriously: the horse and his rider hath he thrown into the sea" (Ex. 15:1). When David defeated the Hittite ruler, Hadadezer, we read that he "houghed [hocked] all the chariot horses, but reserved of them an hundred chariots" (1 Chron. 18:4).

The divine view is suggested in the words of the psalmist, "An horse is a vain thing for safety: neither shall he deliver any by his great strength" (Ps. 33:17). Israel's heartland was largely mountainous, and chariots would be less serviceable than on an open plain. Sisera's chariots had bogged down in the river Kishon's muddy flood plain.

Solomon ignored the stipulation in the law concerning kings and chariots as well as wives and wealth. The chronicler tells us "Solomon gathered together chariots and horsemen: and he had a thousand and four hundred chariots, and twelve thousand horsemen, whom he bestowed in the cities for chariots, and with the king at Jerusalem" (1 Kings 10:26). He was a chariot fancier. He conducted a lucrative trade in horses and chariots from Egypt for the Syrian and Hittite rulers (v. 29). The chronicler includes prices for the horses and chariots, perhaps highlighting the practice as a marker for Solomon's spiritual decline.

The chariot has a less worldly significance in a strange reference preceding its appearance in our story. Among the materials that David gave Solomon along with specifications for the temple furniture was "gold for the pattern of the chariot of the cherubims, that spread out their wings and covered the ark of the covenant of the LORD" (1 Chron. 28:18). Exactly what is indicated by the chariot is unclear, but evidently the chariot, though forbidden for Israel's military uses, was associated with the presence and power of God.

Clearly this is the case when Elisha's servant Gehazi, alarmed by the Syrian army that had compassed the city to take them, was encouraged by God's response to the prayer of his master. "And the LORD opened the eyes of the young man; and he saw: and, behold, the mountain was full of horses and chariots of fire" (2 Kings 6:17). When the Son of God appears in princely gear at the end of time to "judge and make war," He will be riding a white horse for battle (Rev. 19:11).

I see in this incident of Elijah and his successor a suggestion of how we are to conceptualize death. It is a separation and divinely a taking. "Behold, there appeared a chariot of fire, and horses of fire, and parted them both asunder" (2 Kings 2:11). Elisha was left behind. Elijah was gone, "and [Elisha] saw him no more" (v. 12). A loved one had been swept away. There was doubtless painful deprivation, a time of shock and momentarily perhaps of distress and wondering. But notice how quickly the story's focus shifts to the present business of life. "Where *was* the Lord God of Elijah?" must become for the grieving "Where *is* the Lord God of Elijah?" (v. 14) a question to be answered by new stirrings and life empowerment. Elijah's grand exit was Elisha's formal entrance. Elisha was not left without resources. He had been well prepared, and he went immediately into action.

He had the mantle with which to make immediate use. He twisted it into a rod and struck the water, asking, "Where is the Lord God of Elijah?" (v. 14). That had been his master's cry to Israel and summons to Israel's God. Israel's God, in response, would demonstrate His unacknowledged presence. He had not disappeared. Elisha split the water with his mantle as Moses had the Red Sea with his rod. He divided the river as had Joshua and crossed in the same direction. Elisha like his master is associated with their great forerunners in Israel's history. His name in Hebrew, "God saves," is nearly identical with Joshua's, "Jehovah saves." *(Joshua* in Greek is *Jesus,* the name of the Savior.)

Elisha of course had an immediate model, his master's inspiring example. Elijah's transportation from earth becomes for Elisha a metaphor for the old prophet himself. He "saw it, and he cried, My father, my father, the chariot of Israel, and the horsemen thereof" (v. 12). The strength of the nation was concentrated in its "man of God," not in its equipment of war. Two kings, Ahab and Jehoshaphat of Judah, had gone out in chariots to meet Benhadad of Syria with his army and were routed, Ahab mortally wounded. The real defense of Israel was not in the modernity of her armaments but in her faithfulness to the true God.

"The chariot of Israel, and the horsemen thereof" (v. 12) never heard his commendation from his successor. Little would he have credited such high praise during that dreary time in the cave, meditating on what seemed to him a failed life. Elijah could in no way have pictured so triumphant, so life-affirming, a conclusion.

No one could imagine an ending for him, or for any other man, like this one.

We aren't privileged to see the termination of Elijah's grand exit, for it would be an entrance also. In 2 Peter 1:11, Paul writes of an abundant entrance: "An entrance shall be ministered unto you abundantly into the everlasting kingdom of our Lord and Saviour Jesus Christ." We can be confident Paul had no culture shock when he arrived in heaven. And though we can't be an Elijah, that entrance spoken of by Paul is available to us too.

ANOTHER ENTRANCE

Having returned to Gilgal from the region beyond Jordan from which Elijah had first appeared to Ahab, Elisha revisits in reverse order the places the two had passed through before Elijah was separated from him and taken to heaven. At Jericho and Bethel were communities of prophets for whom Elijah and now his successor were their revered heads.

There is an interesting pause in the story in which the "sons of the prophets" (2 Kings 2:15) at Jericho want to be sure that their former master has really been replaced by Elisha. They had already learned the departure was soon to happen and had warned Elisha of it, though he too had known it before. The prophets seem unwilling to accept what they know had been intended by God. They ask Elisha to permit them to search the rugged terrain to be sure "the Spirit of the Lord" has not "taken him up, and cast him upon some mountain, or into some valley" (v. 16).

Their request may have been due to a genuine concern for their former master's safety, but it shows the weakness of their belief in what they had been informed was going to happen (perhaps earlier from Elijah) and certainly an inadequate, even superstitious view of God. (Obadiah had expressed a similar fear in I Kings 18:12.)

Moses had been buried by God on a mountain somewhere also in the region of Moab where no one would know. There would be no grave of either the founder or the reformer of Israel available for a shrine.

After the supernatural crossing of the river Jordan, Elisha performed miracles at Jericho and Bethel, health giving and death dealing respectively, and proceeded to Carmel before returning to Samaria, the capital of northern Israel and evidently his town of residence. We have the sense that a great legacy is being recognized by the successor, who will consummate what the predecessor feared was regrettably left incomplete.

10

ELIJAH REAPPEARS

Just when we think Elijah has left the world scene, we get startled by his reappearance. In the first three Gospels (see Luke 9:28–36), he appears even more grandly than when he left in a chariot of fire. He is seen by Peter, James, and John on "a mountain" (v. 28) conversing with Jesus and Moses. They are talking of Jesus' "decease," in Greek His *exodus*. Elijah is before us again!

Moses, the founder of earthly Israel, and Elijah, its reformer, are in conversation with the Creator and Redeemer of all mankind and the founder of a new Israel based on a new covenant. Elijah was walking in familiar conversation with his successor, Elisha, when the heavenly chariot swept him away. Now he appears in familiar conversation with the One who sent the heavenly chariot and with his predecessor, Moses, who also had passed from the earth without a trace. Jesus like Moses will not escape death but like Elijah will exit dramatically, first from a tomb away from human sight, later from a hill outside Jerusalem in the presence of disciples.

Notice the place of mountains in their great moments for God. Both Elijah and Moses acted for God on mountains. God gave His word physical eminence. The people went up to hear and learn of God. So it would be when on feast days the worshipers would ascend to Jerusalem and within Jerusalem to the temple mount. There God's majesty would envelope also His ministers. Someday those who know the Lord will be, like Moses and Elijah, received into glory and shine like the sun in its glory—like the Son in His glory. Even now they can be in conversation with their Redeemer.

Both Moses and Elijah had down times in their spiritual ministries, but the concluding estimate was entirely positive. They had known the fellowship of their Lord's suffering on earth; here they are participants in the fellowship of His glory. They appear with Jesus in a glorified state, their garments glistening, flashing, with an unbearable radiance. This splendor also awaits the faithful child of God.

FINAL THOUGHTS

This lengthy passage on Elijah's life illustrates what can be learned and understood when one reads Scripture without a specific targeted purpose. To read in this way allows Scripture to come to us with its own intentions, to play upon our minds, and to fully influence us by the very special designs of its great Author.

The wider our field of association from Scripture and the more developed and well-practiced our habit of imaginative reflection, the richer can be the ministry of the Holy Spirit during the space we set aside for the Bible in our minds and our lives.

PART 3

VISUALIZING THE STORY

The whole of Scripture tells a story and meets a diversity of needs. And so it follows that the Bible should be read thoughtfully to envision each divinely inspired account.

Visualizing the story allows for concrete flashes of captivating thought and for entertaining the *whys*, *what elses*, and *what nows* that spring out of the story.

Five examples of such contemplations follow.

11

PSALM 28 AND DAVID'S SLING

I like to think of the twenty-eighth Psalm and others like it in association with David's weapon of choice. In the motion of the sling there is a circling down and back before a thrusting forth of the missile in the pocket. The velocity on release and resulting impact of the missile in the pouch is increased by the reverse direction of the motion. Backward serves forward. Downward serves upward and outward.

Slings were feared weapons not only in ancient times. They are said to have been the only indigenous weapon feared by the Spanish conquistadores. Ancient sources report their accuracy against small targets up to 250 meters. A skilled slinger could select not only a face to strike but a particular part of a face. According to the Greek historian Xenophon, the sling could do damage at 400 meters, its range exceeding that of the bow. These figures may be exaggerated, but the Guinness World Record for projecting a stone by sling is 1,434 feet (approximately 437 meters).

Astrophysicists use what is called "gravity assist" to boost the speed of a space vehicle to the point at which it can escape the gravitational pull of the sun and leave the solar system. Entering the gravitational field of a planet at an angle insufficient to draw it in, the vehicle dramatically accelerates and, circling behind the planet, is whipped out at a speed well exceeding that with which it approached. The technique is known as "the slingshot." Spacecraft possess insufficient power in themselves to escape the gravitational pull of the sun at a speed that will carry them their vast distances. Gravity is made to overcome gravity.

Psalm 28 begins with a servant of God in distress. He is under attack by his enemies, who are also the enemies of God. "Unto thee will I cry, O Lord my rock; be not silent to me: lest, if thou be silent to me, I become like them that go down into the pit. Hear the voice of my supplications, when I cry unto thee, when I lift up my hands toward thy holy oracle" (vv. 1–2). David's situation seems dire, but he knows where to go with it.

He cries to his God, like the author of Lamentations who wrote literally of what David depicts poetically. "I called upon thy name, O Lord, out of the low dungeon" (Lam. 3:55), wrote Jeremiah, associating distress, as in many other Old Testament passages as well as in universal human experience, with a need to be "lifted" up and out.

David's spirits take an upturn about midpoint in the psalm. He praises God for his deliverance. "Blessed be the Lord, because he hath heard the voice of my supplications. The Lord is my strength and my shield; my heart trusted in him, and I am helped: therefore my heart greatly rejoiceth; and with my song will I praise him" (Ps. 28:6–7). The song to which he refers is the present poem, the one he has been writing.

In the closing two verses, the psalmist generalizes his experience into a claim for Israel. He has escaped the clutch of his enemies, the cause of his fears, and his song now rises in celebration of his Deliverer. His Deliverer is Israel's also. "The Lord is their strength, and he is the saving strength of his anointed" (v. 8).

A concluding prayer recognizes the nation's ongoing need for protection and blessing. "Save thy people, and bless thine inheritance: feed them also, and lift them up for ever" (v. 9). What has begun as an urgent prayer for his own deliverance ends in an outpouring of praise of his Deliverer, who can be Israel's as well.

The psalmist has a renewed sense of God's providence. He has taken his reader and listener through an experience (perhaps years before) of desperate need, one which drove him to seek help from the Lord and from which he exited with revived energy and purpose, greater we think than before. Down, back, up and around, and then forward went his spirits to their release point.

The life of our Lord also had its dark descents. He warned His disciples such times would come for them too, especially if they were faithful to their calling and remembered who and what they were. Nor should their spiritual descendants expect to miss the dark times either. The world would be much poorer if what it glimpsed in our lives were only the pleasant times in the life of the Savior. We ourselves would be poorer also.

David's sling—its arc—marks an emotional path for us too. It is a spiritual path for us, as it was for Israel's king.

12

BOX CHECKING

Two stories—one in all three synoptic Gospels, the other only in John—tell of two men of distinction, both rulers, who came to Jesus with a yearning. One had come to the Master from darkness. He had come at night. He came out of the night, but he also had night in his soul. The other came during the day. Yet within him, as we learn, it was also night. Both were drawn to Jesus by a pressing sense of their needs. Their needs turned out to be the same.

Jesus would zero in on their needs. To do so He would have to remove a dangerous error and replace it with the truth they needed. They needed first to be clear about what it was they needed and about what had brought them unwittingly to the solution of their need. Jesus brushed aside their polite words of address and went directly to the business. His opening was abrupt and concussive.

Nicodemus began, "Rabbi, we know that thou art a teacher come from God: for no man can do these miracles that thou doest, except God be with him" (John 3:2). Jesus responded as if He hadn't heard him. His visitor needed to die. He needed to die and be reborn. Only by another birth could he ever see the kingdom of God. That was the need Nicodemus brought with him to the Lord that evening. He had come to learn from the

Master (*Master* here means *teacher*). He was not prepared for the shock and awe.

The young ruler didn't get even that far. Jesus cut him off after his first word. He corrected him as He had Nicodemus at the threshold of what he had made ready to say.

> And when he was gone forth into the way, there came one running, and kneeled to him, and asked him, Good Master, what shall I do that I may inherit eternal life? And Jesus said unto him, Why callest thou me good? There is none good but one, that is, God." (Mark 10:17–18)

Was Jesus denying His deity? Of course not. He was doing two things. The ruler does not recognize whom he is addressing and therefore bungles the protocol. Ordinarily a petitioner in the presence of royalty has been prepped on how to speak. He like Nicodemus did not understand he had come to more than an honored teacher. He was facing a King.

The ruler's petition and subsequent behavior also exhibit another error that springs from the previous one. He does not recognize the truth that, as Paul wrote citing the Old Testament, "There is none righteous, no, not one" (Rom. 3:10). What the ruler intended as a gracious start was profoundly wrong. "If I'm not God, I'm not good," Jesus would have him understand.

I'm not so sure the two visitors were as certain of their religious status as they have sometimes been thought to have been. Why would a Pharisee come to learn from a miracle-working rabbi without elite credentials? What might have prompted a wealthy young ruler (religious? civic?) to run to the "Good Master" and implore, kneeling, how he could gain everlasting life? He had set aside his reputation to get relief on this most troubling of questions. Both had lowered themselves, one literally so, out of respect for the One who could supply them what they needed to know. Let's set Nicodemus aside for now and get on with the young ruler's story.

Of the ruler we are told that Jesus loved him (Mark 10:21). If we are like our Master, we will love him too. To care about this winsome young man is important to our sense of what is about to happen and what happens afterward.

The ruler needed to become like the followers of the Master. He had jumped past that requirement. It was not on his list. So Jesus would show him his list was insufficient. Jesus did not go at his need directly as he had with Nicodemus but came at it in a roundabout way. He was going to let the ruler self-identify. Isn't that the hardest thing for an unbeliever or even a stubborn believer to do? Self-recognition is the start of spiritual change. Jesus would engage him in what I'm going to call *box checking*.

We moderns know a lot about box checking. There is no end it seems of questions to be answered on forms, boxes to be checked yes or no. Medical forms, company reports, job applications, performance reviews at all levels—all are to be expected in the work world where so much depends on data-based decision making. And then there is that stressful box checking at the turn of the year when wage earners like me compare where they were a year ago with where they are now and with where they would like to be.

The village rabbi took the ruler to what was then and is yet the best-known passage in the Mosaic law. The assured young man, wealthy in goods and good deeds, was on his home ground. If he had undergone rabbinic training, he could well have recited by rote the entire Pentateuch. Certainly he would have had drilled into his mind the Decalogue, or Ten Commandments, of Exodus 20. He would also have known Leviticus 19:17–18, the two commandments said by Jesus to sum up the Law.

Jesus' tactic with the ruler is fascinating. Whereas His instruction of Nicodemus was by straightforward lecture, he taught the ruler through engaged learning. The ruler has framed his question about the afterlife in terms of moral status. What must I do, he asked, to inherit eternal life? (Matt. 19:16). Jesus does not directly challenge the ruler's error. He accommodates it in order to correct it: "If thou will enter into life, keep the commandments" (v. 17).

The ruler's responses have a naïve charm: "He saith unto him, Which?" (v. 18). Notice that Jesus does not ridicule him. He gives him boxes to check.

- ❑ Thou shalt do no murder,

- ❑ Thou shalt not commit adultery,

- ❑ Thou shalt not steal,

- ❑ Thou shalt not bear false witness,

- ❑ Honour thy father and thy mother:

- ❑ and, Thou shalt love thy neighbour as thyself. (vv. 18–19)

The ruler replies with the by now expected confidence: "All these things have I kept from my youth up: what lack I yet?" (v. 20).

Again Jesus does not argue with him. In response to the ruler's inquiry about what may remain yet to do, Jesus gives him something to do that will answer his question: "If thou wilt be perfect, go and sell that thou hast, and give to the poor, and thou shalt have treasure in heaven: and come and follow me" (v. 21).

He might have known where Jesus was taking him. Jesus had passed over the first four commandments of the Law about man's relation to God. He had taken him through the last six commandments of the Second Table about the duties of man to man. Or had He? Where in Jesus' list was that last of the six, and of the ten, against coveting?

It was a canny omission by the Master Teacher. The ruler had a blind spot in what had been drilled into his mind from his youth. "Sell all your goods, and give to the poor, and come, follow Me." Jesus had let him answer his own question. He had let him self-indict.

The ruler went away sorrowing. He hadn't counted the cost. He wasn't willing to leave all and follow Christ.

But we aren't through with surprises in this story. Colossians 3:5, listing sins we are to mortify, includes "covetousness, which is idolatry." If covetousness is to be considered idolatry, we have circled back to the First Table of the Law which prohibits false worship. The last command of the six, and of the ten, attaches with the first.

Isn't it intriguing how Jesus' tactics with the ruler and the Pharisee were very much the same? Having dismissed their opening words, He sprung from them, from their very words, what each needed to hear. Isn't it just like God to turn our sincere blunderings to serve His purposes and to minister to our good as well? The young ruler got a tutorial in the worth of good works for salvation. "There is none good but God." Nicodemus learned from the miracle worker about the greatest of miracles, the new birth. The rabbi alone of the two rulers checked that box most important of all.

Jesus went on to speak of the impossibility of a rich person entering the kingdom of heaven and asking whether a camel can pass through the eye of a needle. He answered His own question: "With God all things are possible" (v. 26).

Then it was Peter's turn to speak up, for us and for the rest of the disciples. "Behold, we have forsaken all, and followed thee; what shall we have therefore?" (v. 27). Jesus did not chide Peter for raising the question of payback. He did not say, as we would have said, "Now Peter, you should not be thinking that way. Thoughts of self have no place in My kingdom."

Jesus answered in effect, "A lot!" and did so with emphasis.

> Verily I say unto you, There is no man that hath left house,
> or brethren, or sisters, or father, or mother, or wife, or
> children, or lands, for my sake, and the gospel's, but he
> shall receive an hundredfold now in this time, houses, and
> brethren, and sisters, and mothers, and children, and lands,
> with persecutions; and in the world to come eternal life."
> (Mark 10:29–30)

The Lord never asked His disciples to abandon their good for His. He asked them to relinquish lesser goods for greater. They were to lay up for themselves treasures but in the right place

(Matt. 6:19–20). This to my mind is the greatest surprise of the story.

13

THE KING'S HIGHWAY

Luke introduces his account of the ministry of Christ with a salutation to "most excellent Theophilus" (1:3). We don't know who Theophilus was. The name means "lover of God." Luke says he has "had perfect understanding of all things from the very first" and will present them "in order" (v. 3) to him. Just what Luke meant by "in order" is disputable. Did he mean chronological order or did he mean something else? Matthew began his narrative of the King with a genealogy of Jesus. That would be of special importance to the Jewish, especially rabbinical, mind. Royal lineage was used in determining questions of throne rights, especially the case with a messianic claim. Luke is going to conduct masterfully a narrative that unfolds in argumentative order designed to press upon a universal audience the authority of the Savior of the world.

Luke is going to tell the story of the arrival of the hope of Israel and the hope of the mankind. He begins his beginning with the story of two supernatural births. The first to meet us is Zacharias and Elizabeth's child John. He arrives with prophecy. He will arrive first on the scene later as John the Baptist, calling his nation to repentance. It is his *firstness* that Luke underscores, both in his birth and in his role as herald of the coming King. His message will be one of preparation. It is a call for action. Israel must prepare a highway for a King. A highway is a graded *high* way, evened and elevated for official transit. John takes his comparison from a prophetic passage in Malachi prophesying his role. John's message, like that of his precursor Elijah, is not all that creative. It consists almost entirely of what has been scripted for his role.

Preparing a royal highway is of course metaphorical. It has nothing to do with a road contractor's straightening, elevating, and smoothing of a throughway for official use. It has much to do with the removal of *inner* obstacles. The bulldozing of the *inner* man, making the crooked places straight, blasting boulders into gravel to be hauled away, is an ungrateful thing. The first business in the preparing of a highway of the heart for the entrance of the King—the bulldozing—requires repentance. And that brings us to the episode in Luke 3.

The Baptist's message is an alarm to prepare a royal highway. A great King is on the way and there is much to be done, much that shouldn't have been left this long undone. The nation is sick. It needs shock treatment, and that it will get from John. Repentance is the preparation required for the arrival of the King to His place of rule. Queen Elizabeth the First's frequent visits, "progresses" they were called, to the estates of her wealthy subjects were much anticipated and often dreaded because of the enormous expense of preparing the approach to the house as well as the house itself and lavishly decorating the royal "presence" area where she would sit and receive visitors. It involved a cost that could well bankrupt a wealthy family. So also there is there a bankruptcy—a costly expense—involved in the making ready of a heart for the great King.

John was the prophesied herald of the coming of Israel's king. Luke will make clear eventually that He was not only Israel's king. His throne rights extended further. The King will take up John's message when John has performed his role. The event in Luke chapter 3 follows immediately the story of the boy Jesus. Luke has completed that part of his story of Jesus' beginnings and turns abruptly to the ministry of John. John is an introducer. His message is an introduction to salvation's threshold.

Both John and his message are preparation for the coming of the King.

John gets specific in his warnings. His opening words are blunt, directed toward an undifferentiated multitude but aimed particularly, I think, at the religious frauds: "O generation [offspring] of vipers [snake spawn], who hath warned *you* to flee from the wrath to come?" (Luke 3:7). Why are *you* here? He challenges them not to put confidence in their descent from Abraham. Salvation is a personal—not institutional or cultural—deliverance. Jewish national privilege was probably the greatest barrier to the message of Paul. Is there a counterpart in our day?

Then John starts singling out groups among his audience. Or rather they come in groups in response to his message. He has told the "generation of vipers" to bring forth fruits worthy of repentance. I think this does not imply that works have a contribution to make to their salvation. They are an indicator of the seriousness of the comers. They need to understand the cost. They want to learn the cost. "What shall we do?" they say (v. 10). John will oblige. He will show their areas of defect.

John has distinct words for each group. The first are for "the people" in general. Be unselfish, he says. That strikes to the quick of everyone. Then come the publicans, tax collectors. Don't take more from the people than you're entitled to (v. 13). Forget your personal cut exceeding the required amount. Don't be greedy. Then the soldiers. Don't be cruel. Don't make false charges, perhaps referring to extortion threats. And be content with your wages (v. 14). That circles back to the publican vice. Don't be ungenerous. Don't be dishonest. Don't be greedy. Don't be cruel. Don't complain.

Notice the dos and don'ts. We say that works have nothing to do with salvation. The error of meritorious works for salvation was the great central claim of the Reformers. So what does that message, the gospel message, have to do with what John is telling these members of the crowd to do? It has plenty to do with it.

John is, as noted, an introducer. He has a role to announce the coming of the King. His message is also an introducer. There is a protocol with standards to be respected by visitors to a royal monarch or to our President, like him or not. John is acquainting the multitude with what is expected of them if they are to stand before the King in His presence chamber for His receiving of suppliants. They must have repentant hearts. The rich young ruler turned away. Repentance-free belief is not enough.

John calls for the making ready of the heart for the entrance of the great King.

14

THE ZIKLAG ZIGZAG

The location of Ziklag—a town in the south of Philistia between Gaza on the coast and Beersheba inland—exposed the city to marauding neighboring Amalekites. So when Philistine King Achish of Gath welcomed David and gave him Ziklag, the king likely was thinking David and his six hundred men would help him defend his southern border.

The town figures more largely in David's life than in the geography of the region. You won't normally find it on maps at the back of your Bible. But it gives us a fascinating story, recorded in the last five chapters of 1 Samuel and the first two of 2 Samuel. The death of Saul is central to the story, but this will not be our focus here. We will consider whether David's flight to Philistine country from fear of Saul was a false loop in the divinely purposeful path of his life.

In 1 Samuel 26 David learns that Saul—plus three thousand select troops—is on a mission to capture and kill David, the anointed heir to Saul's reign. They have camped by a hill in the wilderness and are settled for the night. David and Abishai walk into the camp and find Saul and his armor bearer asleep. Abishai tells David that God has delivered Saul into their hands and asks permission to kill him. David rejects his offer and the basis of his offer.

Destroy him not: for who can stretch forth his hand against
the Lord's anointed, and be guiltless? . . . [Either] the Lord
shall smite him; or his day shall come to die; or he shall
descend into battle, and perish. The Lord forbid that I
should stretch forth mine hand against the Lord's anointed.
(1 Sam. 26:9–11)

David takes Saul's spear and canteen of water, then speaks
to the king, shaming him for his unjustified malice. He links
his behavior toward Saul with his desire for God to protect his
own life from Saul. His words seem very close to an expression
of faith.

And, behold, as thy life was much set by this day in mine
eyes, so let my life be much set by in the eyes of the Lord,
and let him deliver me out of all tribulation. (1 Sam. 26:24)

But David's faith, such as it was, falters.

And David said in his heart, I shall now perish one day by
the hand of Saul: there is nothing better for me than that I
should speedily escape into the land of the Philistines; and
Saul shall despair of me, to seek me any more in any coast
[border] of Israel: so shall I escape out of his hand. (1 Sam.
27:1)

He and his men flee to Philistine territory ruled by Achish of
Gath, who warmly receives him. Achish honors David's request
to be given a "place in some town in the country" away from "the
royal city" (v. 5). It was a canny request, framed with humility
but with a purpose in mind. It was not the first time David had
"behaved himself wisely" in the presence of a dangerous king
(1 Sam. 18:14–15, 30). In chapter 28, the tables turn.

David is now safe in Ziklag and is raiding the towns on Philistia's southern border leaving none to publish it in Gath (2 Sam.
1:20). David with his men goes to Gath and offers to fight with
Achish against Israel. Their offer is rejected by the princes of
Achish, as they recall David's victories against them under Saul.

David and his men return to Ziklag to find that their town
has been raided by an Amalekite band and burnt to the ground.
The Amalekites have taken their wives and children along with

everything they owned. David's men turn in their grief against their leader and talk of stoning him.

David seeks the Lord. He asks counsel from the high priest Abiathar—who has the holy ephod—if he should pursue the Amalekites and if he will overtake them. Abiathar tells him yes. David finds the Amalekites enjoying their booty, slaughters them, and reclaims all they took from Ziklag—women and children and material goods, a haul dwarfed by what was collected from their earlier raids.

Meanwhile Saul's depleted army is destroyed by the Philistines at Mount Gilboa, and Saul and his son Jonathan are slain. In 2 Samuel 1, David laments their deaths in splendid poetry (vv. 19–27).

God has now removed the main obstacle to David's anointing as king by Samuel, and David moves his center of action to the ancient patriarchal city Hebron. Here he receives homage from the leaders of Judah and solicits the same from the other tribes.

So was David's flight from Saul a lapse in faith that brought him and his men needless grief? Should it not have happened? It might appear so up close, and who can say finally that it wasn't? But a certain fact—easily overlooked at the end of the account of David's spoiling of the Amalekites—suggests otherwise.

Each of David's followers regained his possessions and evidently a percentage of what was left over, including those men that stayed "by the stuff." David kept the rest. Why? Wasn't that selfish? Wasn't his keeping of the rest unworthy of an aspiring king?

We have what seems an answer to that question that ties in with the larger one of what I have called the Ziglag Zigzag, what we are to make of David's flight to Gath.

> And when David came to Ziklag [after his slaughter of the
> Amalekites], he sent of the spoil unto the elders of Judah,
> even to his friends, saying, Behold a present for you of the
> spoil of the enemies of the LORD; To them which were of
> Bethel, . . . and to them which were in Hebron, and to all

the places where David himself and his men were wont to haunt. (1 Sam. 30:26-31)

The spoil from the Amalekites enabled David to give gifts of gratitude to the leaders of Judah—David's ancestral tribe and the ruling tribe of Israel—and other notables who had befriended David. The gifts—and here is their significance for us today—prompted them to offer David what would become the rule of the nation.

So was Ziklag a zigzag in David's life path? A failure of faith with painful consequences? That's hard to say absolutely. We would have to get into God's wheelhouse and look at His charts to really know. I think we can get some clues from the Psalms David wrote, however. We can also garner some clues for ourselves.

The further we get down the road of our lives the more we can see and the better we can see. What seemed a bent line can later appear straight, or straighter than it seemed at the time. God can give a jerk to a crooked path and make of it a ruler line, or show it capable of becoming such. From Euclidian geometry comes the axiom that the shortest distance between two points is a straight line. From common wisdom comes the truth that the longest way round may be the shortest way home.

My thought is that God has many more scenarios than we can know. He is always slackening and tightening, loosening and reeling in, inserting and extracting to counter our lapses and foolish impulses. The result may not be as elegant a pattern as it could have been. Who is to say?

But we have a great and good God. He is a great weaver of lives. He conducts a life as an orchestra, making shrewd adjustments when something goes wrong, performing damage control as needed. You'll find dissonance here and there in Beethoven and Bach. It results in some of the most gorgeous music we have.

That's not to say that every departure from truth and right is a justifiable one. David had one that most certainly was not, and yet one that God extended from in His larger plan in a positive way. There is redemptive potential in failures of the most absolute kind. We know that truth from the first episode in biblical narrative.

In David's case it seems the Ziklag swerve may not have been a zigzag at all. Or if so, an elegantly managed one. David was providentially restrained from fighting alongside the enemies of God.

A verse ending chapter 26 of 1 Samuel sticks in my mind. I underlined it in my Bible. For me, it points beyond itself, encapsulating the intertwined histories of David and Saul. It resonates with life options. "So David went on his way, and Saul returned to his place" (v. 25). David's way was God's, or would become so because of God's pulling power.

15

THE FATHER'S HAND

What memories do you have of your father's hands? Are they pleasant ones, unpleasant, both? What is dominant? Firm direction, correction? Tender comfort? Thumping praise? A slap on the back? A high-five? Help in a task? A lift from the ground? Instructions for tying shoes? Fixing the car? Turning book pages? Folded when they should be taking direct action?

The hand of Zeus hurled down thunderbolts. Some when they picture their father's hand think of abuse—figurative thunderbolts. How you think of your father may be imaged in how you think of his hands. All these uses have parallels in Scripture with God's engagement in our lives.

Hebrews 12 speaks of the chastening of God. Though His hand is not mentioned, the description is of a father's administering physical correction to his son, purposively and wisely. The passage tells us that God physically corrects, but we understand the author intends not only the physical kind, though that is among His options.

There are many ways God deals with us through disappointment and deprivation. But they are not necessarily the result of our sin. We can stumble from negligence rather than willful disobedience. We can feel God's chastening hand for reasons having nothing to do with our sin at all other than that God is forming us toward what He has in mind for us to become.

Scripture tells us God's motive in His correction of us and what should be our response. Knowing why God sends us unhappiness should help us react in the right way.

Everything turns on our understanding of the difference between judgment and chastening. Chastening is a family thing. Judgment is for those outside the family. Chastening has a constructive purpose. Its motive is love. Its expected response is reverence and acceptance. It has positive results.

> Ye have forgotten the exhortation which speaketh unto you
> as unto children, My son, despise not thou the chasten-
> ing of the Lord, nor faint when thou art rebuked of him:
> For whom the Lord loveth he chasteneth, and scourgeth
> every son whom he receiveth. If ye endure chastening, God
> dealeth with you as with sons; for what son is he whom the
> father chasteneth not? . . . We have had fathers of our flesh
> which corrected us, and we gave them reverence: shall we
> not much rather be in subjection unto the Father of spirits,
> and live? For they verily for a few days chastened us after
> their own pleasure; but he for our profit, that we might be
> partakers of his holiness. (Heb. 12:5–10)

He deals with us in painful ways so that we can be like Him. In a way, that's what good parents do also. They are engaged in life building but especially in character building. They mean for their child to follow good ways like their own.

The result of God's chastening (like the pruning of the vine in John 15) is to that end.

> Now no chastening for the present seemeth to be joyous,
> but grievous: nevertheless afterward it yieldeth the peaceable
> fruit of righteousness unto them which are exercised thereby.
> (Heb. 12:11)

Christian friends and congregation members have a responsibility toward those who are discouraged by their chastening by God, hobbling along, tempted to give up.

> Wherefore lift up the hands which hang down, and the
> feeble knees; And make straight paths for your feet, lest
> that which is lame [has been lamed] be turned out of the

way [lit. put out of joint]; but let it rather be healed. (Heb. 12:12)

How you view the chastening hand of God has a great deal to do with your pace and progress in the Christian life.

This passage in Hebrews speaks to me of the loving hand of God. His hand of chastening sums up a great deal He means me to know of His character and ways and interest in me.

It was another portion of Scripture at the beginning of Revelation that got me thinking in this vein. When you do your Bible reading for the day in a particular place, are other passages also coming to mind? Are your thoughts branching fruitfully?

Revelation opens with a dauntingly severe picture of our Lord. Here we are about to see Him in His role of the world's judge. His main business is judgment, though for the seven churches it will be mingled with chastening. It is a fearsome sight.

I saw seven golden candlesticks; and in the midst of the seven candlesticks one like unto the Son of man, clothed with a garment down to the foot, and girt about the paps with a golden girdle. His head and his hairs were white like wool, as white as snow; and his eyes were as a flame of fire. . . . And he had in his right hand seven stars. . . . And when I saw him, I fell at his feet as dead. (Rev. 1:12–17)

The seven stars we will learn are His messengers to the seven churches of Asia Minor, imaged in the seven candlesticks (or lamps) in the candlestick (or lampstand), the Golden Menora of the Jewish tabernacle and temple. When John saw the One in the midst of the lamps, he "fell at his feet as dead."

The account continues.

And he laid his right hand upon me, saying unto me, Fear not; I am the first and the last. I am he that liveth, and was dead; and, behold, I am alive for evermore. (vv. 17–18)

The hand that held the seven stars rested on John's shoulder. How often might it have rested during those many years before on the shoulders of John and his brother James, those impulsive, unruly, but deeply loyal Sons of Thunder (Mark 3:17)?

Has that hand—your Father's hand—rested on your shoulder? Is it resting there now?

CONCLUSION

The Bible may be read, in fact *should* be read, alive to the purpose with all our intellectual powers engaged. Do not deprive yourself of what writers of stories have always known: that the entire story of Scripture serves serious purpose in powerful ways.

Scripture does indeed contain deep currents. Every piece is carefully fitted into the grand narrative—from separation to restoration, from farness to nearness, from loss to reclamation, with gracious solicitation of fallen beings throughout. Reflective reading draws you into these currents.